ACM SIGCHI
Curricula for Human-Computer Interaction

**ACM Special Interest Group on
Computer-Human Interaction
Curriculum Development Group**

ADVANCING HUMAN CAPABILITIES acm *THROUGH INFORMATION TECHNOLOGY*

This publication is a report of the ACM Special Interest Group on Computer-Human Interaction (SIGCHI) Curriculum Development Group.

Thomas T. Hewett (Drexel University), Chair
Ronald Baecker (University of Toronto)
Stuart Card (Xerox PARC)
Tom Carey (University of Guelph)
Jean Gasen (Virginia Commonwealth University)
Marilyn Mantei (University of Toronto)
Gary Perlman (The Ohio State University)
Gary Strong (Drexel University)
William Verplank (ID Two and Stanford University)

Production Editor: Bill Hefley (Carnegie Mellon University)

The Association for Computing Machinery
1515 Broadway
New York, New York 10036 U.S.A.

ISBN 0-89791-474-0

Additional copies may be ordered prepaid from:

ACM Order Department
P.O. Box 64145 +1-800-342-6626
Baltimore, MD 21264 U.S.A. +1-410-528-4261 (Outside U.S., MD and AK)

ACM Order Number: 608920

Table of Contents

Preface

In August of 1988 the SIGCHI Executive Committee, consisting of Francine Frome, Chair; Phyllis Reisner, Vice Chair; Wendy MacKay, Secretary/Treasurer; and Peter Orbeton, Bulletin Editor, voted to authorize the expenses of a multi-year project to develop a set of curriculum recommendations for education in Human-Computer Interaction. This report presents the work of the Committee assembled to produce those recommendations. Along the way the Curriculum Development Group (CDG) has had several days of face-to-face meetings, a disagreement or two, and more than a moment's frustration with the task which they undertook to grapple with over the period of almost two and one-half years. Volunteers all, the members of the CDG have contributed a considerable amount of time and work to the final production of this report--in some instances as much as two months worth of working days over the course of the project.

Although at one time individuals were identified with different sections of report, by the time it got to its present form the report became truly a group product, having been through several drafts and critiques. Furthermore, the group influence was felt from the very beginning. We engaged in extensive discussion and search for agreement on fundamentals even before electrons were re-routed on the screen of a paper simulator. In addition, over the course of the project we have all reflected upon and been informed by each other's thinking, written work, and visual thinking.

Along with the CDG's efforts, the report has benefited from two separate reviews by members of a Curriculum Advisory Panel (CAP) consisting of: Keith Butler, Boeing Computer Science Group; Bill Buxton, University of Toronto; Steve Cunningham, California State University at Stanislas and SIGGRAPH Education Chair; Jim Foley, Georgia Institute of Technology; Paul Green, University of Michigan; Rex Hartson, Virginia Polytechnic and State University; David Kieras, University of Michigan; Jakob Nielsen, Bellcore and formerly of the Technical University of Denmark; Don Norman, University of California at San Diego; Dan Olsen, Jr., Brigham Young University; Judy Olson, University of Michigan; Jenny Preece, The Open University, UK; Ben Shneiderman, University of Maryland; John Thomas, NYNEX; Gerrit van der Veer, The Free University of Amsterdam, The Netherlands; John Whiteside, DEC; and Russel Winder, University College London, UK and BCS HCI SG Liaison. The CAP commented on and critiqued one or more earlier versions of this report and served as a useful counterbalance for the CDG. We all knew they were watching over our shoulders, metaphorically if not literally. As you might expect, members of the CAP did not always agree with some of the things we said or with some of our fundamental assumptions. Nonetheless, we have been quite careful in attending to what they told us, especially where we chose not to modify our assumptions or the contents of the report in response to their comments.

In addition to the CAP, several other people contributed to the final report. Individuals who deserve special mention for their willingness to do a close reading of the penultimate draft of the report and provide thoughtful comments on relatively short notice are Izak Benbasat, University of British Columbia; Jonathan Grudin, University of California, Irvine; Aaron Marcus, Aaron Marcus Associates; Lawrence Miller, The Aerospace Corporation; Don Patterson, Lawrence Livermore National Laboratory; and Thomas Sheridan, M.I.T. At both CHI '89 and CHI '90 the CDG organized a Special Interest Group Session on Curriculum Development and were gratified and enlightened by the helpful and supportive comments of those who attended. In some cases CAP members asked junior colleagues or senior graduate students to provide comments on an earlier draft. Finally, almost 50 people spontaneously volunteered to read and comment on the penultimate version of the report. Although all of these people have not been named here, we truly appreciate their time and thank them for their efforts.

In conclusion, there are two important points which need to be stressed and which will be mentioned again later in the report. First, the CDG has attempted to create an heuristic structure with which, and within which, others can work to improve the state of education in Human-Computer Interaction. Given that one of our explicit goals was to avoid being prescriptive we have offered an inventory of things known about the field, a set of sample course descriptions which represent possible mappings of that content into course structures, and a set of sample curriculum descriptions. These exemplars are just that, examples. In each case they are but one of a family of mappings which could have been created. They are intended to make it possible for others to analyze their own local conditions and create their own unique mappings.

Second, the CDG members consider the results presented in this report to be the first iteration in the design of a product which is intended to have a long course of future iterative refinement and development, refinement of both the exemplar courses and the curricula. In fact, being convinced of the importance of the process of iterative design and evaluation of product, and recognizing the rapid pace with which the technology of HCI is changing, it is our sincere hope that in this report we have sown the seeds of the obsolescence of our own recommendations. We invite you to keep the best of our work, to discard our mistakes, and to create an improved product.

Tom Hewett, Chair, ACM SIGCHI CDG

CHAPTER 1

Introduction

Over the last twenty years, computer science has developed rapidly as a discipline. As the content of computer science has continued to evolve and gain new substance, the curriculum of computer science has continually been revised to reflect the new content and deeper understandings of the nature of computers and information. This active reorganization is as would be expected for a new, vigorously developing discipline.

The Association for Computing Machinery and the IEEE Computer Society, as the primary scientific/professional computer societies, have taken a leading role in the development of model curricula for computer science (ACM 1968, 1977, 1979; Denning, *et al.*, 1988; IEEE Computer Society, 1976, 1983; ACM/IEEE-CS Joint Curriculum Task Force, 1991). Carnegie-Mellon University has also published a curriculum and its rationale (Shaw, 1985). As computer science curricula have developed, human-computer interaction (HCI) has, with other topics, gradually become a part of many of the curricula. For example, the Carnegie-Mellon curriculum report cited has a course in interface design, a collateral psychology course in human factors, and integrates human-computer interaction topics as appropriate in several courses (e.g., Languages, Interfaces, and their Processors). The recent ACM report on the core of computer science (Denning, *et al.*, 1988), includes human-computer communication as one of nine subareas comprising computer science. Human-computer interaction topics are a part of this area as are topics in computer graphics.

Human-computer interaction itself has over the last 10-15 years emerged as a focus research area with specialist organizations:

- The ACM Special Interest Group on Computer Human Interaction
- The British Computer Society Specialist Group on HCI
- The IFIP Technical Committee (TC 13) on Human-Computer Interaction
- The Human Factors Society Computer Systems Technical Group
- The European Association for Cognitive Ergonomics

specialist journals:

- *Human-Computer Interaction*
- *International Journal of Man-Machine Studies*
- *Behavior and Information Technology*
- *International Journal of Human-Computer Interaction*
- *Interacting with Computers*

and specialist conferences:

- ACM CHI Human Factors in Computing Systems Conference
- ACM User Interface Software Technology Conference
- BCS HCI SG Human-Computer Interaction Conference
- European Conference on Cognitive Ergonomics
- IFIP INTERACT Human Factors in Computing Conference
- International Conference on Human-Computer Interaction

New research results have been generated from this focus. There has, however, been a shortage of educational materials for preparing courses in human-computer interaction. An ACM workshop on curricula in human-computer interaction was held in 1985 (Mantei, 1985) and several instructors have published descriptions of their courses (e.g., Green, 1984; Hewett, 1987a; Hix, 1990; Perlman, 1989; Strong, 1989; Verplank & Kim, 1987). The current level of activities and the development of studies in human-computer interaction is far enough along that the next step in developing educational programs is now possible. The time is appropriate to attempt initial inventories of the field and to make recommendations for education in human-computer interaction. To attempt such an exercise, the ACM Special Interest Group in Computer-Human Interaction (SIGCHI) created a Curriculum Development Group in August, 1988. The task of the committee was to produce a set of recommendations for education in human-computer interaction.

This is the report from that committee. The committee included members primarily from universities, but also members with experience in industrial organizations. All members had taught courses in this area and most were faculty regularly teaching such courses. In addition, most of the members of the group have, at one time or another, been actively engaged in the process of interactive software development and evaluation.

The committee had six face-to-face meetings over the course of two years. To gather input from the community of people interested in the teaching of human-computer interaction, the CDG solicited input through the *SIGCHI Bulletin*, organized two open SIG meetings at the CHI '89 and CHI '90 conferences on Human Factors in Computing Systems, conducted a tutorial session for CHI '91, worked with a curriculum advisory panel of 17 leading researchers in the field from Europe and North America, and, during the later stages of report preparation, recruited a large number of volunteer reviewers from a wide variety of career and educational backgrounds. These people provided feedback on various drafts of the curriculum document.

The following sections of the report detail our recommendations and rationale for teaching human-computer interaction in a university setting. Chapter 2 gives a working definition of human-computer interaction and its relationship to other bodies of knowledge. Chapter 3 details example designs for individual courses and, along with Chapter 4, lays out a basic approach to HCI education, the student populations we address, the educational programs, and how HCI fits into the curriculum. In addition, Chapter 4 proposes example curricula. The final chapter of the report, Chapter 5, discusses some of the educational issues raised by our recommendations and tries to identify the report's limitations and unresolved issues.

The Appendices serve as resources for individuals wishing to develop HCI education at their institution. Appendix A is a section on "Getting Started," and recommends books, journals, videos and other relevant materials to support possible courses. Appendix B lays out the curriculum of an Information Systems Program. Appendix C lists a curriculum that has been put in place in a Computer Science department. Appendix D describes an existing interdisciplinary curriculum. Each of these existing curricula differs from the suggested "ideal" curricula being recommended because of the political and resource constraints of its sponsoring institution, but in each case there is a strong conceptual relationship to the proposals in Chapter 4. Appendix E contains resource material from a sample university course that has been taught in HCI. This course is an undergraduate computer science course and the materials include syllabi, assignments, and examinations. Appendix F contains sample case studies from industry projects in HCI which can be used in the classroom.

Overall, this document is intended to be a resource for anyone wishing to put together either a single course or a program in human-computer interaction. The goal has been to avoid being prescriptive and to offer a structure which is flexible enough that individuals in differing environments can adapt, modify, and supplement the basic report and its recommendations in ways which are suitable for the environment in which they must work. Feedback on the contents of the report should be directed to the ACM SIGCHI Education Chair, ACM, 1515 Broadway, New York, NY 10036.

CHAPTER 2

Human-Computer Interaction

2.1 Definition of HCI

There is currently no agreed upon definition of the range of topics which form the area of human-computer interaction. Yet we need a characterization of the field if we are to derive and develop educational materials for it. Therefore we offer a working definition that at least permits us to get down to the practical work of deciding what is to be taught:

> *Human-computer interaction is a discipline concerned with the design, evaluation and implementation of interactive computing systems for human use and with the study of major phenomena surrounding them.*

From a computer science perspective, the focus is on *interaction* and specifically on interaction between one or more *humans* and one or more computational *machines*. The classical situation that comes to mind is a person using an interactive graphics program on a workstation. But it is clear that varying what is meant by *interaction*, *human*, and *machine* leads to a rich space of possible topics, some of which, while we might not wish to exclude them as part of human-computer interaction, we would, nevertheless, wish to identify as peripheral to its focus. Other topics we would wish to identify as more central.

Take the notion of *machine*. Instead of workstations, computers may be in the form of embedded computational machines, such as parts of spacecraft cockpits or microwave ovens. Because the techniques for designing these interfaces bear so much relationship to the techniques for designing workstations interfaces, they can be profitably treated together. But if we weaken the computational and *interaction* aspects more and treat the design of machines that are mechanical and passive, such as the design of a hammer, we are clearly on the margins, and generally the relationships between humans and hammers would not considered part of human-computer interaction. Such relationships clearly *would* be part of general human factors, which studies the human aspects of all designed devices, but not the mechanisms of these devices. Human-computer interaction, by contrast, studies both the mechanism side and the human side, but of a narrower class of devices.

Or consider what is meant by the notion *human*. If we allow the human to be a group of humans or an organization, we may consider interfaces for distributed systems, computer-aided communications between humans, or the nature of the work being cooperatively performed by means of the system. These are all generally regarded as important topics central within the sphere of human-computer interaction studies. If we go further down this path to consider job design from the point of view of the nature of the work and the nature of human satisfaction, then computers will only occasionally occur (when they are useful for these ends or when they interfere with these ends) and human-computer interaction is only one supporting area among others.

There are other disciplinary points of view that would place the focus of HCI differently than does computer science, just as the focus for a definition of the databases area would be different from a computer science vs. a business perspective. HCI in the large is an interdisciplinary area. It is emerging as a specialty concern within several disciplines, each with different emphases: computer science (application design and engineering of human interfaces), psychology (the application of theories of cognitive processes and the empirical analysis of user behavior), sociology and anthropology (interactions between technology, work, and organization), and industrial design (interactive products). In this report, we have adopted, as an ACM committee, an appropriate computer science point of view, although we have tried at the same time to consider human-computer interaction broadly enough that other disciplines could use our analysis and shift the focus appropriately. From a computer science perspective, other disciplines serve as supporting disciplines, much as physics serves as a supporting discipline for civil engineering, or as mechanical engineering serves as a supporting discipline for robotics. A lesson learned repeatedly by engineering disciplines is that design problems have a context, and that the overly narrow optimization of one part of a design can be rendered invalid by the broader context of the problem. Even from a direct computer science perspective, therefore, it is advantageous to frame the problem of human-computer interaction broadly enough so as to help students (and practitioners) avoid the classic pitfall of design divorced from the context of the problem.

To give a further rough characterization of human-computer interaction as a field, we list some of its special concerns: Human-computer interaction is concerned with the joint performance of tasks by humans and machines; the structure of communication between human and machine; human capabilities to use machines (including the learnability of interfaces); algorithms and programming of the interface itself; engineering concerns that arise in designing and building interfaces; the process of specification, design, and implementation of interfaces; and design trade-offs. Human-computer interaction thus has science, engineering, and design aspects.

Regardless of the definition chosen, HCI is clearly to be included as a part of computer science and is as much a part of computer science as it is a part of any other discipline. If, for example, one adopts Newell, Perlis, and Simon's (1967) classic definition of computer science as "the study of computers and the major phenomena that surround them," then the interaction of people and computers and the uses of computers are certainly parts of those phenomena. If, on the other hand, we take the recent ACM (Denning, *et al.*, 1988) report's definition as "the systematic study of algorithmic processes that describe and transform information: their theory, analysis, design, efficiency, implementation, and application," then those algorithmic processes clearly include interaction with users just as they include interaction with other computers over networks. The algorithms of computer graphics, for example, are just those algorithms that give certain experiences to the perceptual apparatus of the human. The design of many modern computer applications inescapably requires the design of some component of the system that interacts with a user. Moreover, this component typically represents more than half a system's lines of code. It is intrinsically necessary to understand how to decide on the functionality a system will have, how to bring this out to the user, how to build the system, how to test the design.

Because human-computer interaction studies a human and a machine in communication, it draws from supporting knowledge on both the machine and the human side. On the machine side, techniques in computer graphics, operating systems, programming languages, and development environments are relevant. On the human side, communication theory, graphic and industrial design disciplines, linguistics, social sciences, cognitive psychology, and human performance are relevant. And, of course, engineering and design methods are relevant.

2.2 Field of HCI

The goal of this section is to provide background for this report in terms of some of the major themes and influences that have shaped the field of HCI. In addition, an attempt is made to project some current trends into the near future as a basis for anticipating some of the conditions with which students will be faced upon, or even before, graduation. This section is not intended to provide either an exhaustive history of the past or a full scale "futures projection." It is, rather, to provide a context for the recommendations which follow.

2.2.1 Historical Roots

Human-computer interaction arose as a field from intertwined roots in computer graphics, operating systems, human factors, ergonomics, industrial engineering, cognitive psychology, and the systems part of computer science. Computer graphics was born from the use of CRT and pen devices very early in the history of computers. This led to the development of several human-computer interaction techniques. Many techniques date from Sutherland's Sketchpad Ph.D. thesis (1963) that essentially marked the beginning of computer graphics as a discipline. Work in computer graphics has continued to develop algorithms and hardware that allow the display and manipulation of ever more realistic-looking objects (e.g., CAD/CAM machine parts or medical images of body parts). Computer graphics has a natural interest in HCI as "interactive graphics" (e.g., how to manipulate solid models in a CAD/CAM system).

A related set of developments were attempts to pursue "man-machine symbiosis" (Licklider, 1960), the "augmentation of human intellect" (Engelbart, 1963), and the "Dynabook" (Kay and Goldberg, 1977). Out of this line of development came a number of important building blocks for human-computer interaction. Some of these building blocks include the mouse, bitmapped displays, personal computers, windows, the desktop metaphor, and point-and-click editors (see Baecker & Buxton, 1987, Chapter 1).

Work on operating systems, meanwhile, developed techniques for interfacing input/output devices, for tuning system response time to human interaction times, for multiprocessing, and for supporting windowing environments and animation. This strand of development has currently given rise to "user interface management systems" and "user interface toolkits".

Human factors, as a discipline, derives from the problems of designing equipment operable by humans during World War II (Sanders & McCormick, 1987). Many problems faced by those working on human factors had strong sensory-motor features (e.g., the design of flight displays and controls). The problem of the human operation of computers was a natural extension of classical human factors concerns, except that the new problems had substantial cognitive, communication, and interaction aspects not previously developed in human factors, forcing a growth of human factors in these directions. Ergonomics is similar to human factors, but it arose from studies of work. As with human factors, the concerns of ergonomics tended to be at the sensory-motor level, but with an additional physiological flavor and an emphasis on stress. Human interaction with computers was also a natural topic for ergonomics, but again, a cognitive extension to the field was necessary resulting in the current "cognitive ergonomics" and "cognitive engineering." Because of their roots, ergonomic studies of computers emphasize the relationship to the work setting and the effects of stress factors, such as the routinization of work, sitting posture, or the vision design of CRT displays.

Industrial engineering arose out of attempts to raise industrial productivity starting in the early years of this century. The early emphasis in industrial engineering was in the design of efficient manual methods for work (e.g., a two-handed method for the laying of bricks), the design of specialized tools to increase productivity and reduce fatigue (e.g., brick pallets at waist height so bricklayers didn't have to bend over), and, to a lesser extent, the design of the social environment (e.g., the invention of the suggestion box). Interaction with computers is a natural topic for the scope of industrial engineering in the context of how the use of computers fit into the larger design of work methods.

Cognitive psychology derives from attempts to study sensation experimentally at the end of the 19th century. In the 1950's, an infusion of ideas from communications engineering, linguistics, and computer engineering led to an experimentally-oriented discipline concerned with human information processing and performance. Cognitive psychologists have concentrated on the learning of systems, the transfer of that learning, the mental representation of systems by humans, and human performance on such systems.

Finally, the growth of discretionary computing and the mass personal computer and workstation computer markets have meant that sales of computers are more directly tied to the quality of their interfaces than in the past. The result has been the gradual evolution of a standardized interface architecture from hardware support of mice to shared window systems to "application management layers." Along with these changes, researchers and designers have begun to develop specification techniques for user interfaces and testing techniques for the practical production of interfaces.

2.2.2 Likely Future Developments

The means by which humans interact with computers continues to evolve rapidly. A curriculum in a changing area must be put together with some understanding of the forces shaping the future so that its concepts are not quickly out of date. Although the curriculum can always be revised in the light of greater understanding in the future, students cannot generally be recalled for retraining. They must build their own future understanding upon the foundations provided by the courses taken at the time they were students.

Human-computer interaction is, in the first instance, affected by the forces shaping the nature of future computing. These forces include:

- Decreasing hardware costs leading to larger memories and faster systems.
- Miniaturization of hardware leading to portability.
- Reduction in power requirements leading to portability.
- New display technologies leading to the packaging of computational devices in new forms.
- Assimilation of computation into the environment (e.g., VCRs, microwave ovens, televisions).
- Specialized hardware leading to new functions (e.g., rapid text search).
- Increased development of network communication and distributed computing.
- Increasingly widespread use of computers, especially by people who are outside of the computing profession.
- Increasing innovation in input techniques (e.g., voice, gesture, pen), combined with lowering cost, leading to rapid computerization by people previously left out of the "computer revolution."
- Wider social concerns leading to improved access to computers by currently disadvantaged groups (e.g., young children, the physically/visually disabled, etc.).

Because human-computer interaction involves transducers between humans and machines and because humans are sensitive to response times, viable human interfaces are more technology-sensitive than many parts of computer science. For instance, the development of the mouse gave rise to the point-and-click style of editor interface and the mouse-based graphics program. Partially based on the above trends, we expect a future for HCI with some of the following characteristics:

- *Ubiquitous communication*. Computers will communicate through high speed local networks, nationally over wide-area networks, and portably via infrared, ultrasonic, cellular, and other technologies. Data and computational services will be portably accessible from many if not most locations to which a user travels.

- *High functionality systems.* Systems will have large numbers of functions associated with them. There will be so many systems that most users, technical or non-technical, will not have time to learn them in the traditional way (e.g., through thick manuals).
- *Mass availability of computer graphics.* Computer graphics capabilities such as image processing, graphics transformations, rendering, and interactive animation will become widespread as inexpensive chips become available for inclusion in general workstations.
- *Mixed media.* Systems will handle images, voice, sounds, video, text, formatted data. These will be exchangeable over communication links among users. The separate worlds of consumer electronics (e.g., stereo sets, VCRs, televisions) and computers will partially merge. Computer and print worlds will continue to cross assimilate each other.
- *High-bandwidth interaction.* The rate at which humans and machines interact will increase substantially due to the changes in speed, computer graphics, new media, and new input/output devices. This will lead to some qualitatively different interfaces, such as virtual reality or computational video.
- *Large and thin displays.* New display technologies will finally mature enabling very large displays and also displays that are thin, light weight, and have low power consumption. This will have large effects on portability and will enable the development of paper-like, pen-based computer interaction systems very different in feel from desktop workstations of the present.
- *Embedded computation.* Computation will pass beyond desktop computers into every object for which uses can be found. The environment will be alive with little computations from computerized cooking appliances to lighting and plumbing fixtures to window blinds to automobile braking systems to greeting cards. To some extent, this development is already taking place. The difference in the future is the addition of networked communications that will allow many of these embedded computations to coordinate with each other and with the user. Human interfaces to these embedded devices will in many cases be very different from those appropriate to workstations.
- *Group interfaces.* Interfaces to allow groups of people to coordinate will be common (e.g., for meetings, for engineering projects, for authoring joint documents). These will have major impacts on the nature of organizations and on the division of

labor. Models of the group design process will be embedded in systems and will cause increased rationalization of design.

- *User Tailorability.* Ordinary users will routinely tailor applications to their own use and will use this power to invent new applications based on their understanding of their own domains. Users, with their deeper knowledge of their own knowledge domains, will increasingly be important sources of new applications at the expense of generic systems programmers (with systems expertise but low domain expertise).
- *Information Utilities.* Public information utilities (such as Compuserve, Prodigy, home banking and shopping, etc.) and specialized industry services (e.g., weather for pilots) will continue to proliferate. The rate of proliferation will accelerate with the introduction of high-bandwidth interaction and the improvement in quality of interfaces.

One consequence of the above developments is that computing systems will appear partially to dissolve into the environment and become much more intimately associated with their users' activities. One can make an analogy to the development of motion power. Once, strikingly visible, large, centralized water wheels were used to drive applications via belt drives; now electric motors are invisibly integrated into applications from VCRs to refrigerators.

Of course, personal computers in some form will continue to exist (although many might take the form of electronic notebooks) and there will still be the problem of designing interfaces so that users can operate them. But the rapid pace of development means that the preparation of students must address not only the present state of technology, but also provide the foundations for future possibilities.

2.3 The Content of Human-Computer Interaction

The aim in this section is to inventory the current state of results in the field of human-computer interaction. Our object is to delimit the scope of our concerns and to specify the connections with other fields. The discussion is not constrained by the need to distribute this content into courses or to tailor a curriculum for various sorts of students. The objective is, rather, to survey what is known that is worth teaching. Different courses might be carved out of parts of this inventory, and the program at a particular school or in any given instructional environment might wish to utilize only part of this material, together with other topics in a reorganized point of view (e.g., for a course in a design department or for a short, in-house training course for members of product development teams). For convenience, we have loosely arranged the topics in the field into 16 groups (Table 1).

The topics in this table derive from a consideration of five interrelated aspects of human-computer interaction: (N) the nature of human-computer interaction, (U) the use and context of computers, (H) human characteristics, (C) computer system and interface architecture, and (D) the development process. Although not content areas, *per se*, and not discussed in the inventory below, project presentations and examinations (P) have been included as a category in this table to stress the importance of having students be exposed to content both through lecture and through the process of actually working on course projects, and in recognition of the fact that in most instructional environments some sort of evaluation of student mastery of content is necessary.

Some of the interrelationships among these topics are represented in Figure 1 on page 16. Computer systems exist within a larger social, organizational and work milieu (U1). Within this context there are applications for which we wish to employ computer systems (U2). But the process of putting computers to work means that the human, technical, and work aspects of the application situation must be brought into fit with each other through human learning, system tailorability, or other strategies (U3). In addition to the use and social context of computers, on the human side we must also take into account the human information processing (H1), communication (H2), and physical (H3) characteristics of users. On the computer side, a variety of technologies have been developed for supporting interaction with humans: Input and output devices connect the human and the machine (C1). These are used in a number of techniques for organizing a dialogue (C2). These techniques are used in turn to implement larger design elements, such as the metaphor of the interface (C3). Getting deeper into the machine substrata supporting the dialogue, the dialogue may make extensive use of computer graphics techniques (C4).

TABLE 1. Content of HCI

CONTENT AREAS		
N	The Nature of HCI	
	N1	(Meta-)Models of HCI
U	Use and Context of Computers	
	U1	Human Social Organization and Work
	U2	Application Areas
	U3	Human-Machine Fit and Adaptation
H	Human Characteristics	
	H1	Human Information Processing
	H2	Language, Communication, Interaction
	H3	Ergonomics
C	Computer System and Interface Architecture	
	C1	Input and Output Devices
	C2	Dialogue Techniques
	C3	Dialogue Genre
	C4	Computer Graphics
	C5	Dialogue Architecture
D	Development Process	
	D1	Design Approaches
	D2	Implementation Techniques
	D3	Evaluation Techniques
	D4	Example Systems and Case Studies
P	Project Presentations and Examinations	

Complex dialogues lead into considerations of the systems architecture necessary to support such features as interconnectable application programs, windowing, real-time response, network communications, multi-user and cooperative interfaces, and multi-tasking of dialogue objects (C5). Finally, there is the process of development which incorporates design (D1) for human-computer dialogues, techniques and tools (D2) for implementing them (D2), techniques for evaluating (D3) them, and a number of classic designs for study (D4). Each of these components of the development process is bound up with the others in a relationship of

FIGURE 1. **Human-Computer Interaction**

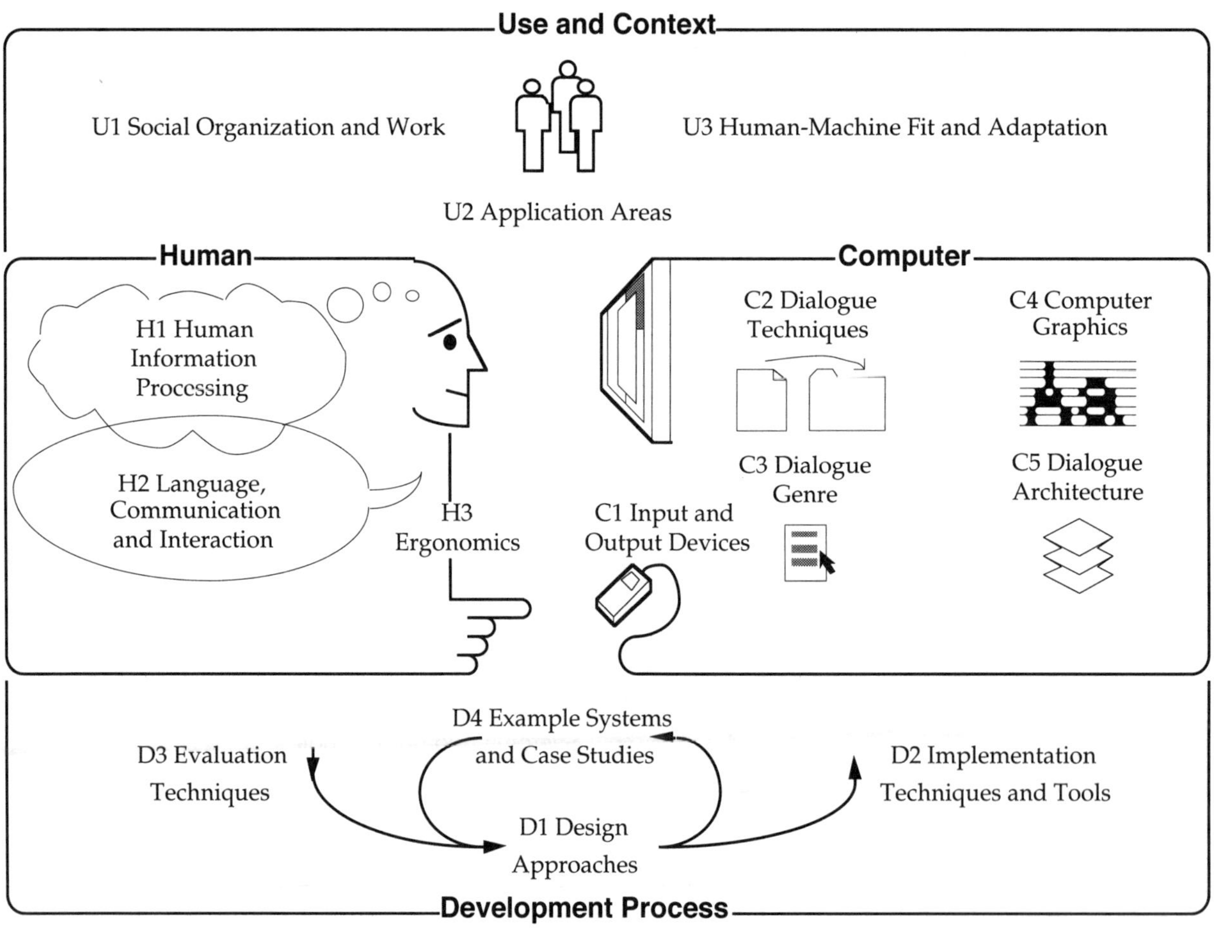

mutual, reciprocal influence whereby choices made in one area impact upon the choices and the options available in the others.

The following inventory of topics contains representative entries relating to all of these aspects of the design and analysis of human-computer interaction systems. This inventory is a current snapshot of topics on which there are results that could be taught. In addition to direct HCI topics, we have included in this inventory results from other disciplines central enough to be taught within courses in HCI. Such a list cannot hope to be complete or even non-controversial, but it should be heuristically useful in the practical business of preparing courses.

2.3.1 Nature of Human-Computer Interaction (N)

Under this heading are overviews of, and theoretical frameworks for, topics in human-computer communication.

N1. The Nature of Human-Computer Interaction

Points of view: HCI as communication, agent paradigm, tool paradigm, the work-centered point of view, human/system/tasks division, supervisory control

Objectives (e.g. productivity, user empowerment)

History and intellectual roots

HCI as an academic topic: journals, literature, relation to other fields, science vs. engineering vs. design aspects

2.3.2 Use and Context of Computers (U)

The uses to which computers are put are spoken of as 'applications' in the computer world. These uses and the extent to which the interface (and the application logic in the rest of the system) fits them can have a profound impact on every part of the interface and its success. Moreover, the general social, work, and business context may be important. In addition to technical requirements, an interface may have to satisfy quality-of-work-life goals of a labor union or meet legal constraints on "look and feel" or position the image of a company in a certain market. The following topics are concerned with general problems of fitting computers, uses, and context of use together.

U1. Social Organization and Work

This heading relates to the human as an interacting social being. It includes a concern with the nature of work, and with the notion that human systems and technical systems mutually adapt to each other and must be considered as a whole.

Points of view (e.g., industrial engineering, operations research, Rasmussen's cognitive engineering, the Aarhus participatory design approach, Hewitt's open systems)

Models of human activity (e.g., opportunistic planning, open procedures)

Models of small-groups, organizations

Models of work, workflow, cooperative activity, office work

Socio-technical systems, human organizations as adaptive open systems, mutual impact of computer systems on work and vice versa, computer systems for group tasks, case studies

Quality of work life and job satisfaction

U2. Application Areas

The focus of this section is on classes of application domains and particular application areas where characteristic interfaces have developed.

Characterization of application areas (e.g., individual vs. group, paced vs. unpaced)

Document-oriented interfaces: Text-editing, document formatting, illustrators, spreadsheets, hypertext

Communications-oriented interfaces: Electronic mail, computer conferencing, telephone and voice messaging systems

Design environments: programming environments, CAD/CAM

On-line tutorial systems and help systems

Multimedia information kiosks

Continuous control systems: process control systems, virtual reality systems, simulators, cockpits, video games

Embedded systems: Copier controls, elevator controls, consumer electronics and home appliance controllers (e.g., TVs, VCRs, microwave ovens, etc.)

U3. Human-Machine Fit and Adaptation

Part of the purpose of design is to arrange a fit between the designed object and its use. There are several dimensions to this fit and it is possible to place the burden of adjustment in different places: Adjustments can be made (1) either at design time or at time of use (2) by either changing the system or the user and (3) the changes can be made by either the users themselves or, sometimes, by the system. Topics under this heading all relate to changing some component of a socio-technical system so as to improve its fit.

Alternate techniques for achieving fit

Nature of adaptive systems, adaptations of human systems that cancel reliability improvements, the nature of error in adaptive redundant systems, empirical findings on user improvisation with routine systems, determinants of successful systems introduction,

System selection: theories of system adoption

System adaptation: customization and tailorability techniques

User selection: compatibilities of user and system characteristics

User adaptation: ease of learning, training methods (e.g., on-line tutorials), relation to system design

User guidance: help techniques, documentation, error-handling techniques

2.3.3 Human Characteristics (H)

It is important to understand something about human information-processing characteristics, how human action is structured, the nature of human communication, and human physical and physiological requirements.

H1. Human Information Processing

Characteristics of the human as a processor of information.

Models of cognitive architecture: symbol-system models, connectionist models, engineering models

Phenomena and theories of memory

Phenomena and theories of perception

Phenomena and theories of motor skills

Phenomena and theories of attention and vigilance

Phenomena and theories of problem solving

Phenomena and theories of learning and skill acquisition

Phenomena and theories of motivation

Users' conceptual models

Models of human action

Human diversity, including disabled populations

H2. Language, Communication and Interaction

Language as a communication and interface medium. Communication phenomena.

Aspects of language: syntax, semantics, pragmatics

Formal models of language

Pragmatic phenomena of conversational interaction (e.g., turn-taking, repair)

Language phenomena

Specialized languages (e.g., graphical interaction, query, command, production systems, editors)

Interaction reuse (e.g., history lists)

H3. Ergonomics

Anthropometric and physiological characteristics of people and their relationship to workspace and environmental parameters.

Human anthropometry in relation to workspace design

Arrangement of displays and controls, link analysis

Human cognitive and sensory limits

Sensory and perceptual effects of CRT and other display technologies, legibility, display design

Control design

Fatigue and health issues

Furniture and lighting design

Temperature and environmental noise issues

Design for stressful or hazardous environments

Design for the disabled

2.3.4 Computer System and Interface Architecture (C)

Machines have specialized components for interacting with humans. Some of these components are basically transducers for moving information physically between human and machine. Other components have to do with the control structure and representation of aspects of the interaction. These specialized components are covered in the following topics.

C1. Input and Output Devices

The technical construction of devices for mediating between humans and machines.

Input devices: survey, mechanics of particular devices, performance characteristics (human and system), devices for the disabled, handwriting and gestures, speech input, eye tracking, exotic devices (e.g., EEG and other biological signals)

Output devices: survey, mechanics of particular devices, vector devices, raster devices, frame buffers and image stores, canvases, event handling, performance characteristics, devices for the disabled, sound and speech output, 3D displays, motion (e.g., flight simulators), exotic devices

Characteristics of input/output devices (e.g., weight, portability, bandwidth, sensory modality)

Virtual devices

C2. Dialogue Techniques

The basic software architecture and techniques for interacting with humans.

Dialogue Inputs:

Types of input purposes (e.g., selection, discrete parameter specification, continuous control)

Input techniques: keyboard techniques (e.g, commands, menus), mouse-based techniques (e.g., picking, rubber-band lines), pen-based techniques (e.g., character recognition, gesture), voice-based techniques

Dialogue Outputs:

Types of output purposes (e.g., convey precise information, summary information, illustrate processes, create visualizations of information)

Output techniques (e.g., scrolling display, windows, animation, sprites, fish-eye displays)

Screen layout issues (e.g., focus, clutter, visual logic)

Dialogue Interaction Techniques:

Dialogue type and techniques (e.g., alphanumeric techniques, form filling, menu selection, icons and direct manipulation, generic functions, natural language)

Navigation and orientation in dialogues, error management

Multimedia and non-graphical dialogues: speech input, speech output, voice mail, video mail, active documents, videodisc, CD-ROM

Agents and AI techniques

Multi-person dialogues

Dialogue Issues:

Real-time response issues

Manual control theory

Supervisory control, automatic systems, embedded systems

Standards

"Look and feel," intellectual property protection

C3. Dialogue Genre

The conceptual uses to which the technical means are put. Such concepts arise in any media discipline (e.g., film, graphic design, etc.).

Interaction metaphors (e.g., tool metaphor, agent metaphor)

Content metaphors (e.g., desktop metaphor, paper document metaphor)

Persona, personality, point of view

Workspace models

Transition management (e.g., fades, pans)

Relevant techniques from other media (e.g., film, theater, graphic design)

Style and aesthetics

C4. Computer Graphics

Basic concepts from computer graphics that are especially useful to know for HCI.

Geometry in 2- and 3- space, linear transformations

Graphics primitives and attributes: bitmap and voxel representations, raster-op, 2-D primitives, text primitives, polygon representation, 3-D primitives, quadtrees and octtrees, device independent images, page definition languages

Solid modeling, splines, surface modeling, hidden surface removal, animation, rendering algorithms, lighting models

Color representation, color maps, color ranges of devices

C5. Dialogue Architecture

Software architectures and standards for user interfaces.

Layers model of the architecture of dialogues and windowing systems, dialogue system reference models

Screen imaging models (e.g., RasterOp, Postscript, Quickdraw)

Window manager models (e.g., Shared address-space, client-server), analysis of major window systems (e.g., X, New Wave, Windows, Open Look, Presentation Manager, Macintosh)

Models of application-to-dialogue manager connection

Models for specifying dialogues

Multi-user interface architectures

"Look and feel"

Standardization and interoperability

2.3.5 Development Process (D)

The construction of human interfaces is both a matter of design and engineering. These topics are concerned with the methodology and practice of interface design. Other aspects of the development process include the relationship of interface development to the engineering (both software and hardware) of the rest of the system.

D1. Design Approaches

The process of design. Relevant topics from other design disciplines.

Graphic design basics (e.g., design languages, typography, use of color, 2D & 3D spatial organization, temporal sequencing, etc.)

Alternative system development processes (e.g., waterfall model, participatory design), lifecycle model, iterative design, choice of method under time/resource constraint

Task analysis techniques (e.g., field studies, analytical methods), task allocation, market analysis

Design specification techniques

Design analysis techniques (e.g., objects and actions)

Industrial design basics

Design case studies and empirical analyses of design

D2. Implementation Techniques and Tools

Tactics and tools for implementation.

Relationships among design, evaluation, and implementation

Independence and reusability, application independence, device independence

Prototyping techniques (e.g., storyboarding, video, "Wizard of Oz", HyperCard, rapid prototype implementations)

Dialogue toolkits (e.g., MacApp, NextStep, UIMS's, HyperCard)

Object-oriented methods

Data representation and algorithms

D3. Evaluation Techniques

Philosophy and specific methods for evaluations.

Productivity

Figures of merit (e.g., time, errors, learnability, design for guessing, preference, etc.)

Usability testing techniques, linking testing to specifications

Formative and summative evaluation techniques for empirical evaluation, including, field observation methods, participant observation, interviewing techniques, questionnaire design, psychometric methods, video protocols, system logging, experiment design (e.g, concern with sample bias, etc.), methods from psychological and sociological evaluation fields, ethics of working with participants

D4. Example Systems and Case Studies

Classic designs to serve as extended examples of human interface design.

Command-oriented:

OS/360 JCL (batch-oriented command style, baseline for seeing later improvements)

PC DOS (command style interface learned by millions)

Airline check-in system (time pressure, ambiguous input, distributed system)

Graphics-oriented:

Xerox Star (icon-window interface, generic commands)

Apple Macintosh (similar interface over many applications)

MacPaint (widely known and available graphics program)

Frame-based:

Promis (Rapid response to large set of frames, touch-panel oriented)

Zog (User-tailorable, rapid-response system, large number of frames, first commercial frame-based system)

HyperCard (Graphically-oriented frame-based system with user programming language, first mass market frame-oriented system).

User-defined combinatorics:

Unix operating system (strong combinatoric architecture paired with weak human factors)

Emacs (language-oriented, large combinatoric command set)

Visicalc (a "home-run" application with strong conceptual model that succeeded despite weak human factors)

DBaseIII (simple, but successful, user applications generator)

Interfaces for untrained, walk-up users:

Olympic Message System (practical use of user testing under time pressure)

Nintendo Super Mario Brothers (learnable without a manual by grade school children)

The topics listed in this chapter constitute an attempt to inventory the results of HCI and its supporting fields that are available for teaching. The topics are not arranged according to how they would appear in courses. Rather, they are the raw material out of which courses and curricula might be fashioned and recommendations for such courses and curricula are provided in Chapters 3 and 4. However, HCI as a field is continuing to develop rapidly. It is expected, therefore, that the above topics will undergo change as new results occur and as our understanding of the area deepens. New paradigms will emerge as our fundamental concepts evolve, become more clearly articulated, and spin off entirely new subtopics. These changes will necessitate continual revision of courses and curricula as new topics and results emerge.

CHAPTER 3

Courses in HCI

In informal discussions with our advisory panel and with people attending SIGCHI conference special interest group meetings on HCI education, there was a recurring request for help in preparing a first and perhaps a second course on HCI, much more so than for a detailed curriculum. In this chapter, we make recommendations for introductory courses in HCI. Our work draws upon experiences teaching a variety of courses in many departments. The result consists of four course designs, based on a mapping of the content of HCI outlined in Chapter 2 into course structures designed for particular audiences. Given our ACM SIGCHI charter, we directed our initial attention to courses that could be offered in a computer science department, but given the multidisciplinary background of the CDG, we also discussed courses that could be offered to students from other departments, especially psychology, human factors, or industrial and systems engineering departments. Finally, we have tried to provide for the fact that those individuals working in a teaching environment which differs markedly from the one envisioned here may need to instantiate a different course, or courses, by suitable modification of the order and the relative balance of topics in one or more of our proposed courses, or by judicious picking and choosing from the content inventory to shorten or lengthen the course. In other words, each course recommendation is intended to be a representative of a family of possible courses which might be fashioned from the content inventory provided in Chapter 2.

3.1 The Four Proposed Courses

Table 2 relates the content of HCI and the emphases of each topic for each of four proposed courses. This table also reflects the compromises in goals and philosophy of the members of the Curriculum Development Group, and requires some explanation. For different types of students, different orientations are necessary. The proposed courses can be broadly characterized as either technology oriented (CS1: User Interface Design and Development and CS2: Phenomena and Theories of Human-Computer Interaction) or human oriented (PSY1: Psychology of Human-Computer Interaction and MIS1: Human Aspects of Information Systems), and as moving from a general professional/practical orientation (CS1 and MIS1) to one that is more specialized and research oriented (CS2 and PSY1).

CS1 and CS2. The first two courses are the ones that would most probably be offered as a sequence in a computer science department, but they could be offered in a more general information systems department or in a more specialized software engineering department. The CS1 course (User Interface Design and Development) stresses practical software development concepts and would be a natural complement to a software engineering course or program. CS1 also focuses on how students in a computer discipline, notably software engineering, can produce better user interfaces. It has a major project that requires that students work on design, implementation (using tools like window libraries and UIMSs), and practical evaluation methods with their artifact, with a major goal being the realization that user interfaces are demonstrably imperfect and can be improved.

The CS2 course (Phenomena and Theories of Human-Computer Interaction) looks at HCI in a broader context, focusing on the phenomena and theories of HCI, and is intended for students interested in specializing in HCI. In CS2, the design and evaluation techniques are more refined, and there is a greater emphasis on scientific foundations of HCI. A design/implementation/evaluation project in this course begins with less well-defined requirements than in CS1 (User Interface Design and Development). The project requires that students focus more on users and on task analysis.

TABLE 2. Course Emphases on the Content of HCI

CONTENT AREAS (course length assumed to be 14 weeks with 42 contact hours total)		CS1: UI Design & Devel.	CS2: Phen & Thy of HCI	PSY1: Psych of HCI	MIS1: Human Aspects of IS
N	The Nature of HCI				
	N1 (Meta-)Models of HCI	2	2	2	1
U	Use and Context of Computers				
	U1 Human Social Organization and Work	2	4	4	4
	U2 Application Areas	1	1	1	4
	U3 Human-Machine Fit and Adaptation	2	2	4	3
H	Human Characteristics				
	H1 Human Information Processing	1	9	4	1
	H2 Language, Communication and Interaction	1	5	2	2
	H3 Ergonomics	1	2	1	1
C	Computer System and Interface Architecture				
	C1 Input and Output Devices	2	0	3	2
	C2 Dialogue Techniques	3	0	4	3
	C3 Dialogue Genre	1	0	1	1
	C4 Computer Graphics	1	0	1	1
	C5 Dialogue Architecture	1	0	1	0
D	Development Process				
	D1 Design Approaches	4	2	4	4
	D2 Implementation Techniques	5	2	2	4
	D3 Evaluation Techniques	5	6	4	3
	D4 Example Systems and Case Studies	3	2	2	4
P	Project Presentations and Examinations	7	5	2	4

PSY1. The Psychology of Human-Computer Interaction course might be offered in a psychology, human factors, or industrial engineering department. It stresses the theoretical and empirical foundations of the field much more than the courses based in computer science. The course design presented here assumes this to be the only HCI course available to students. It also assumes that students have the prerequisites of human information processing psychology (especially cognitive) and a background in applied statistics (especially experimental design, data collection and analysis). It takes this knowledge and applies it to HCI, with special emphasis on design and evaluation techniques particularly relevant to HCI. Although implementation *per se* is not a major component of the course, tools such as HyperCard should be used as a design/implementation prototyping environments to allow evaluation and redesign to begin during the early stages of design/ implementation.

MIS1. The Human Aspects of Information Systems course is designed to give professional non-technically oriented users (and managers of users) a better understanding of the HCI issues in the systems with which they interact. End-users must make decisions on which systems to buy and use, and the purpose of this course is, in effect, to increase consumer awareness of issues. Understanding the role of computers in organizations and how to evaluate the suitability of technological solutions is a major emphasis. Although not thought of as system builders, many students in this course may well become involved in program design and implementation with widespread tools like spreadsheets and databases, both of which have considerable prototyping and programming capability.

3.2 Sequencing Courses

In a computer discipline, the CS1 course (User Interface Design and Development) might well be the first and perhaps the only course taken by many students. However, for more advanced study and a broader perspective, students would take CS2 (Phenomena and Theories of Human-Computer Interaction) as the second in a sequence. Similarly, if a version of all of the proposed courses actually existed on a single campus, then students coming from a psychological discipline would probably begin with PSY1 (Psychology of Human-Computer Interaction), and then move on to the CS2 course (Phenomena and Theories of Human-Computer Interaction) which has less emphasis on implementation than does CS1 (User Interface Design and Development). However, if both CS1 and CS2 were offered as a sequence many computer science departments would be hard-pressed to find resources or even faculty for both courses. There are potential solutions to this problem.

For example, given the broader perspective of CS2 (Phenomena and Theories of Human-Computer Interaction), it might well be based in a different department than CS1 (User Interface Design and Development) and cross listed (as is the case for a few similar courses currently offered in some institutions). Alternatively, if one could arrange to coordinate an HCI course in a computer discipline with an HCI course in a psychological discipline, those two courses could be a lot like CS1 and PSY1 (Psychology of Human-Computer Interaction), but with the relative balance of material in the former being shifted to include more emphasis on Computer System and Interface Architecture topics, and with the relative balance of material in the latter being changed to increase the emphasis on Human Characteristics topics while decreasing the emphasis on Computer System and Interface Architecture topics.

Other Specialization Courses. In instructional environments where there is a rich concentration of expertise in HCI, one could also envision a spectrum of advanced level courses that would be of benefit to students. For example, the students who have completed PSY1 (Psychology of Human-Computer Interaction) might profit from a special topics *HCI Laboratory* course in which the main focus was on the foundational empirical research work on HCI. The more research-oriented students in a computer discipline might also move on to the HCI Laboratory course after completing CS2 (Phenomena and Theories of Human-Computer Interaction), whereas the more development oriented students might better be offered an HCI Project course after completing CS2.

After having completed either CS1 (User Interface Design and Development) or CS2 (Phenomena and Theories of Human-Computer Interaction), it would also be appropriate for interested students in a computer discipline to take on more advanced courses on topics such as User Interface Specification and User Interface Management Systems, Window Systems, or Hypertext Engineering. After having completed PSY1 (Psychology of Human-Computer Interaction), it would be appropriate for interested students to take a course on topics such as Cognitive Engineering, Theoretical Models of Human-Computer Interaction, or Computer Supported Cooperative Work. Given the orientation of MIS1 (Human Aspects of Information Systems) students whose primary interests and goals are satisfied by such a course are not seen as taking other specialist courses in HCI.

Multidisciplinary Courses. As a *capstone experience,* it should also be possible to have students from both computer and psychological disciplines combining their complementary skills in a course HCI Practicum which combines the goals of the HCI Project and the HCI Laboratory courses and which would challenge the students from different backgrounds to apply their education and skills and learn to work in project groups during the design and development of a usable and useful interactive software project. In some institutions it may also be possible to involve students from film, video, and the graphic design disciplines as well. Naturally, the sequence that such students would follow would depend heavily on the specific course content at a university.

Integrating HCI Into Existing Courses. Although we are not making specific recommendations for integrating HCI into existing courses, we recommend that in general the mention of major important HCI topics and issues be incorporated into all technology oriented courses. Too often, the only evaluative component of software engineering, for example, is the testing of the correctness of software or the analysis of performance, while ignoring the impact of user misconceptions and user efficiency. When a user makes a mistake, the correctness of some software may not be relevant, and any investments of time and money in the efficiency of the software can be lost many times over as a result of loss of user productivity. For these important reasons, we recommend that iterative design, usability testing and user productivity be at least mentioned as issues of concern in courses at all levels, along with the traditional complementary issues in software engineering. The goals are to develop in students an appreciation for the importance of HCI issues in the overall acceptance and success of interactive software and to offer them pointers to appropriate courses.

3.3 Structure of the Course Descriptions

This section provides a description of the generic structure and common background for each recommended course. Each description, with a title and alternate title, will have the following parts:

1. a general **course catalog description**;

2. **students and prerequisites** describe who might take the course, in what department(s), and what skills and knowledge they should have in preparation;

3. **philosophy and objectives** explain what we think the student should get out of the course;

4. a **content** outline with level of treatment (emphasis) matched to topics in Table 3.1, with terminology (knowledge units) matched to that in Chapter 2 of this report;

5. an implied schedule geared for a course with 14 3-hour weeks; and

6. a short set of suggested **resources**, materials and/or sources of information for teaching the specific course (these sections are very brief and intended primarily to provide a flavor for the type of material and to serve as pointers into Appendix A: Resources for Human-Computer Interaction).

All of these courses share several traits in common. Rather than repeat all of a core set of objectives, prerequisites, *etc.* for each course, we have listed the shared traits here to emphasize the aspects common to the four courses in HCI proposed here.

Shared Objectives of the Courses. By taking courses in HCI, we expect students to have gained an understanding of the following:

o *the scope of issues affecting human-computer interaction*
o *the importance of the user interface* to motivate the study of topics like HCI and user interfaces

- o *the impact of good and bad user interfaces*
- o *the diversity of users and tasks (applications)* and their impact on the design of user interfaces
- o *the limits of knowledge of individuals* developing HCI systems
- o *the need to work with others,* skilled in diverse areas such as software engineering, human factors, technical communication, statistics, graphic design, etc.
- o *cost/benefit trade-offs in HCI design*
- o *different system development lifecycles* including those particularly applicable to HCI systems (e.g., iterative design, implementation, evaluation, and prototyping)
- o *how HCI concerns can be incorporated into systems development lifecycles*
- o *the need to evaluate system usability* (e.g., someone will evaluate usability even if not the developer, and, in some cases, not evaluating constitutes professional misconduct)
- o *the existence of design, implementation, and evaluation tools* for developers with diverse needs and technical expertise
- o *the information sources available on HCI*

Shared Prerequisites for the Courses. We don't expect that every institution will have an existing program meeting all desired prerequisites. Indeed, the HCI courses must contribute their share to developing some of these generic topics. Customizing the course frameworks may therefore include replacing some of the recommended HCI material with units in these areas. Conversely, some programs will cover some of the recommended HCI material in prerequisite or co-requisite courses - e.g., in a computer graphics course. All students taking the proposed courses should:

- o *be advanced undergraduates or beginning graduate students*
- o *have the ability to write clearly for a general audience*
- o *have the experience and skills for working in teams*
- o *have experience with different levels of computer support for the same task* (e.g., use of a text editor vs. a word-processor for creating documents)
- o *have some programming experience and considerable experience using computers*
- o *have at least one course in applied statistics*

o *have a course in psychology, preferably human information processing* (although this may be unrealistic)

Shared Goals for Coverage of Content. In the course descriptions which follow, it is assumed that the instructors will have and set certain specific and specifiable goals in coverage of the content. Those goals can and should be stated in terms of desired learning outcomes which describe the level of understanding and experience students are expected to achieve. The major goals we believe to be important are:

o *Definition:* students can recognize and recall terminology, facts and principles For example, students can define 'direct manipulation' and list some of its strengths and weaknesses as an interaction style.

o *Concept Understanding*: students can determine the relationships between specific instances and broader generalizations. For example, students can determine which parts of a system exhibit direct manipulation features and can explain why a change in the system produced different properties.

o *Directed Application*: students can use concepts and principles to explain, analyze and solve specific situations, often with the applicable concepts implicit in the setting. For example, students can redesign part of an interface to exhibit direct manipulation style and predict the likely effects of the change.

o *Realistic Problem Solving:* students can apply course content in coping with real life situations. These differ from directed applications by having less structured questions and issues, no direction as to which concepts will be applicable and a range of potentially acceptable answers. For example, students can design an interface for real tasks and users which incorporates direct manipulation in appropriate ways (and evaluate/defend their choices).

Common Suggestions for Schedules and Exercises. A number of people (e.g., Hewett, 1987b; Mantei, 1985) have made teaching suggestions for encouraging active student involvement in learning about HCI issues, some of which are highlighted below:

- o *Protocol gathering*
- o *Field observations*
- o *Analysis and evaluation* of sample interfaces
- o *Design* (not necessarily construction) of an interface
- o *Case studies*
- o *Teaching people to use a system*
- o *Running evaluations* with live or prototype systems, or paper and pencil scenarios
- o *Iterative paper writing* on design (modified every two weeks)
- o *Creative thinking exercises* on analogies for design
- o *Discussion groups,* debates on design trade-offs
- o *Design team* projects or competitions
- o *Field trips* to businesses or research centers supporting various user interface systems
- o *Guest lecturers*
- o *Videotape* interviews or observations of new, unique systems

General Resources for the Courses. There is no single source of information (e.g., textbook) useful for teaching all or even one of the proposed courses. The collection by Baecker and Buxton (1987) is comprehensive, thought provoking, and affordable. Collections of high-quality chapters are found in Salvendy (1987) and Helander (1989). The Software Engineering Institute at Carnegie-Mellon University has published a curriculum module with support materials on user interface development (Perlman, 1989). While this curriculum module is not a textbook, it is a teacher's resource for almost any course in HCI, particularly User Interface Design and Development, because of its detailed annotated content outline and categorical bibliography.

3.4 Course Descriptions

This section addresses the specific design of each of the four recommended courses (CS1, CS2, PSY1 and MIS1). Each course description contains a sample course catalog description, some comments about the assumed students and prerequisites, a statement of the philosophy and objectives for each course, and a topical listing of course content. This topical listing is keyed to the inventory in Chapter 2 by notations such as "D3:4," which means "Topic D3 gets 4 lecture hours."

3.4.1 CS1: User Interface Design and Development

Course Catalog Description: CS1 stresses the importance of good interfaces and the relationship of user interface design to human-computer interaction. Other topics include: interface quality and methods of evaluation; interface design examples; dimensions of interface variability; dialogue genre; dialogue tools and techniques; user-centered design and task analysis; prototyping and the iterative design cycle; user interface implementation; prototyping tools and environments; I/O devices; basic computer graphics; color and sound.

Students and Prerequisites: This course is intended for students in computing disciplines (computer science and software engineering) whose work may interact with user interface issues. We believe that this represents all computer science students and that therefore this course should be required for all students graduating with a degree in computer science or software engineering. In addition to the prerequisites mentioned earlier, students are expected to have considerable experience using computers. They are also expected to understand the non-HCI specific areas of the following topics:

- *needs analysis and requirements definition for computing systems*
- *software development* (including design, implementation, testing, debugging and documentation)
- *software engineering* (especially the scaling-up problems from individual student efforts to long-term software systems built by software teams)

Philosophy and Objectives: Graduates in computing are usually expected to have professional skills which can be put to work relatively quickly, so this first course is intended to provide an adequate basis in software design and implementation for user interfaces. There is content on both the issues and engineering process for user interfaces. This course also includes an appreciation of the importance of further subjects covered in CS2 (Phenomena and Theory of Human-Computer Interaction). Students will learn:

- o *How HCI relates to other aspects of software engineering*, and that HCI requires additional design skills and knowledge
- o *Basic skills and knowledge for user interface design* and will understand some of the limitations of their knowledge. The basic knowledge will include the features of interaction styles and devices and their relationship to user characteristics
- o *At least one development methodology and one toolkit* for prototyping/implementing user interfaces, and awareness of other methods and tools that are available

One of the key requirements for organizing the content of the course is to enable students to quickly begin project work. This implies covering evaluation material early in the semester and sequencing the design and implementation content to precede the related part of the design project. Material not directly applicable on the project may be included towards the end of the course, in parallel with the last project stage.

Course Content:

1. Introduction to the course (N1:1) (1 hour)

   Examples illustrating the importance of user interface design

   The relationship of the discipline of user interface design to the science of human-computer interaction

2. Interface quality and evaluation (D3:4) (4 hours)

   Measures of user interface quality

   Methods for observation and evaluation

3. Interactive system and interface design examples (U2:1, D4:2) (3 hours)

Examples such as word processors, spreadsheets, hypertext systems, programming environments, ATM's, voice answering systems and mail systems

4. Dimensions of interface variability (H2:1, C2:3, C3:1, U3:2) (7 hours)

   Languages, communication and interaction

   Dialogue genre; the role of metaphor

   Dialogue techniques (including windows, menus, icons, etc.)

   User support and assistance, documentation, training

5. User-centered design and task analysis (D1:4, U1:2, D4:1) (7 hours)

   Software engineering design models, user-centered design, participatory design

   Socio-technical issues

   Task analysis

   Prototyping and the iterative design cycle; the evolution of designs

   The role of principles and guidelines

   Examples of designs

6. User interface implementation (D2:5, C1:2, C4:1, C5:1, H3:1) (10 hours)

   Prototyping tools and environments

   Input and output devices

   Ergonomic issues

   Basic results from computer graphics

   Interface modalities: color, sound, etc.

The role of graphic and industrial design

Toolkits and interface development environments, e.g., window managers, UIDE's

7. Evaluation revisited; learning from HCI research; the role of models (D3:1, H1:1) (2 hours)

    A deeper look at evaluation

    Learning from HCI research; applying science to interface design

    Human information processing models and their role

8. System and interface design project: presentations and discussion (spread throughout term) (P:5) (5 hours)

9. Course summary and wrap-up; interfaces of the future (N1:1) (1 hour)

10. Examinations (P:2) (2 hours)

Resources:

Baecker, R. M. & Buxton, W. A. S. (1987). *Readings in Human-Computer Interaction*. San Mateo CA.: Morgan Kaufmann Publishers.

Heckel, P. (1982). *The Elements of Friendly Software Design*. New York: Warner Books.

Laurel, B. (1990). *The Art of Human-Computer Interface Design*. Reading, Mass.: Addison-Wesley Publishing Company.

Perlman, G. (1988). Teaching User Interface Development to Software Engineers. *Proceedings of the Human Factors Society - 32nd Annual Meeting*, 391-394.

Perlman, G. (1990). Teaching User Interface Development to Software Engineering and Computer Science Majors. *ACM SIGCHI Bulletin*, 22 (1), 61-66.

3.4.2 CS2: Phenomena and Theories of Human-Computer Interaction

Course Catalog Description: CS2 is designed to train the computer science student in how to apply the theories of HCI to the task of design. It surveys the techniques available in the discipline, demonstrates where and when they are applicable and proceeds to demonstrate via a combination of scientific theory understanding and engineering modeling, and the solution of design problems facing a user interface designer.

The course surveys a wide range of psychological theories beginning with organizational behavior approaches to understanding work and workflow within organizations and moving to understanding human psychological architecture and processing constraints. It also covers new design methods and techniques available and the new conceptual mechanisms used in HCI such as the metaphors for describing user interaction.

Students and Prerequisites: As mentioned earlier, it is intended that the students in this course are either advanced undergraduates or beginning graduate students. As a prerequisite they will have taken either the CS1 course (User Interface Design and Development), the PSY1 course (Psychology of Human-Computer Interaction), or the equivalent of one of those courses.

Philosophy and Objectives: This course is intended for students from computer science, and other disciplines, who expect all or part of their future professional work to be devoted to the development of user interfaces. It's intent is to train students in the underlying science and its application to user interface design. It is an engineering course replete with engineering models drawn from psychological theory. The course trains the student in when and where to apply what models to solve specific design problems. Where theory is not robust, apprenticeship training is employed, demonstrating to students what to look for in user behavior and what design changes different forms of problematic behavior suggest. Since the science of HCI is an evolving science, the course is also a resources course which points the way to acquiring continuing information on the field and also lays a groundwork for understanding future applied research papers in the field. What the course does not teach is how to do HCI science, i.e., how to use basic psychological theory and experimentation to develop new engineering models. Its focus is on the use and adaptation of existing theory and research to a range of new problems a user interface designer faces.

Course Content:

1. Introduction to the science of HCI (N1:2) (2 hours)

   The specific disciplines that comprise HCI

   Information and solutions provided by each discipline

2. The development process (D1:1) (1 hour)

   Alternative system development processes

   Inclusion of HCI discipline in the development process

3. Social organization and work (U1:4) (4 hours)

   Small group dynamics

   Theory of networks

   Organizational information flow

   Models of work, workflow and cooperative activity

   Impact on design

4. Methodology (D3:3) (3 hours)

   Methods for capturing, analyzing and applying data at the organizational and social level of human behavior

   Problems of validity

   Questionnaire design

   Conducting surveys

   Unobtrusive measures

5. Human-machine fit and adaptation (U3:2) (2 hours)

Nature and theory of adaptive systems

Theories of system adoption and methodology used to ascertain and motivate adoption

User adaptation: ease of learning, training methods

System adaptation to user types

Relationship to system design

6. The Human Information Processor (H1:9) (9 hours)

    Description of human architecture and performance of critical subunits (e.g., memory, perception, motor skills, etc.)

    Models of human activity (e.g., GOMS models, Keystroke Level model, etc.)

    Applications of model human information processor to example problems

7. Application areas in human-computer interaction: a survey of relevant problems and characteristics (U2:1) (1 hour)

8. Languages, Communication and Interaction (H2:5) (5 hours)

    Aspects of Language

    Formal models of language

    Language phenomena

    Pragmatic phenomena of conversational interaction

    Specialized languages (e.g., query, production systems, etc.)

9. Ergonomics (H3:2) (2 hours)

    Arrangement of displays and controls, link analysis

    Control design

    Design for disabilities

Fatigue and health issues

10. Design specification techniques (D1:1) (1 hour)

    Methods for describing the interface (e.g., design specification, design analysis, etc.)

    Application of task analyses

11. Implementation techniques (D2:2) (2 hours)

    Prototyping tools and trade-offs

12. Evaluating the design (D3:3) (3 hours)

    Conducting and analyzing usability studies

13. Case studies of the development and introduction of specific interfaces (D4:2) (2 hours)

14. Special Project and Examinations (P:5) (5 hours)

    Sample Project (Running throughout the course with lectures devoted specifically to its support):

    Design and implement a prototype system. First, using questionnaires, interviews and unobtrusive observation, obtain and evaluate the initial design information. Next, create a paper design, followed by modeling and evaluation of the design with the human information processing model. Finally, do prototyping and user testing of the design, followed by redesign and improvement based upon the information gained.

Resources:

Many books would be needed to introduce the broad content of this course. The collection of Baecker and Buxton (1987) would be a good source of readings, as would readings from chapters of Salvendy (1987) and Helander (1989). To introduce human information processing psychology, Lindsay and Norman (1977) would be adequate and lively, while Kantowitz and Sorkin (1983) would contain more applied material. To make students think about measurement and statistics, and to introduce concepts of experimental design, the following two little books have proven themselves.

Campbell, S. K. (1974). *Flaws and Fallacies in Statistical Thinking*. Englewood Cliffs, NJ: Prentice-Hall.

Solso, R. L. & Johnson, H. H. (1984). *An Introduction to Experimental Design in Psychology: A Case Approach*, (3rd Edition). New York: Harper & Row.

3.4.3 PSY1: Psychology of Human-Computer Interaction

Course Catalog Description: This applied course is both a survey of Human-Computer Interaction research and an introduction to the psychological and other behavioral science knowledge and techniques useful in the design of computing systems for human use. Particular emphasis is placed on developing a knowledge of the basic psychological phenomena of human cognition, memory, problem solving and language, and on how those processes relate to and condition the interaction between humans and interactive computing systems.

Students and Prerequisites: As noted in the prerequisites mentioned earlier, the students in this course are expected to come from psychology or a related behavioral science and to be advanced undergraduates or beginning graduate students. They might also be computer science majors taking the course as an elective.

Philosophy and Objectives: There are three major objectives for this course. One objective is to familiarize students with some of the basic human and machine related factors that influence the design and development of interactive computing systems. A second objective is to familiarize students with current theory and research on the psychological factors to be considered in designing interactive computing systems. The third objective for the course is to explore the interrelationships between psychological processes and the characteristics of computing systems being designed for human use, and, in so doing, to develop an appreciation for the ways in which theory and research can guide design and in which design experience can contribute to the development of theory and research.

Course Content:

1. Nature of HCI (N1:2) (2 hours)

    Objectives of course and HCI

    History and intellectual roots

    Human system task division

    HCI as communication

    Agent paradigm

    Tool paradigm

    Work-centered point of view

2. Human Information Processing (H1:4, H2:2, H3:1) (7 hours)

    Human cognitive and sensory limits

    User's conceptual models (mental models)

    Models of cognitive architecture

    Human memory

    Human problem solving

    Aspects of language: syntax, semantics, pragmatics

3. Computer System and Interface Architecture (C1:3, C2:4, C3:1, C4:1, C5:1) (10 hours)

    Input and Output devices: survey, mechanics of particular devices, performance characteristics (human and system), speech input, sound and speech output

    Dialogue input and output techniques and purposes

    Screen layout issues

Dialogue interaction: types and techniques, navigation and orientation, multimedia and non-graphical dialogues

Dialogue issues: response time, control, standards, look and feel

Use of abstract metaphors for describing interface behavior

Use of metaphors to support user understanding

Statistical models for describing interaction processes

Computer graphics

Color representation, color maps, color range of devices

Layers model of architecture of design and windowing systems

Windows manager models, e.g., X, Macintosh, MS Windows

4. Use and Context of Computers (U1:4, U2:1, U3:4) (9 hours)

Points of view: Industrial engineering, participatory management, Rasmussen's cognitive engineering

Open procedures, a la Suchman (1987)

Models of small groups and organizations

Models of work and cooperative activity

Socio-technical systems: mutual impact of systems on work and vice versa, computer systems for group tasks, workflow

Quality of work life and job satisfaction

Electronic mail

Text editing and/or spreadsheets

Multimedia information kiosks

Nature of adaptive systems: system selection and adaptation, user selection and adaptation

Alternative techniques for achieving fit

5. Development Process (D1:4, D2:2, D3:4, D4:2) (12 hours)

Industrial design basics

System development process

Iterative design

Task analysis techniques

Design analysis and specification, e.g., objects and actions a la Newman & Sproull (1972)

Relationships between evaluation, design, implementation, and testing

Prototyping techniques

Figures of merit

Usability testing

Evaluation techniques

6. Examinations (P:2) (2 hours)

Resources:

Card, S. K., Moran, T. P. & Newell, A. (1983). *The Psychology of Human Computer Interaction*. Hillsdale, NJ: Lawrence Erlbaum Associates.

Green, P. (1990). Readings on Human Factors in Computer Systems: The 1989 List. *ACM SIGCHI Bulletin*, *21*(4), 20-26.

3.4.4 MIS1: Human Aspects of Information Systems

Course Catalog Description. Human-computer interaction for professionals, managers and information systems specialists.

Analysis and design of systems from the point of view of HCI. Focus on selecting and using information systems to support human work. Emphasis placed on user involvement in the development process.

Students and Prerequisites. The intended audience includes individuals from any number of disciplines such as information systems, anthropology, sociology, graphic design, film and video, management, other business concentrations, English, engineering, or psychology. As mentioned earlier, students should have completed a course in psychology, preferably cognitive psychology or human information processing, and have some computer programming or end-user computing experience.

Philosophy and Objectives. Students will be able to identify and understand the:

- variety of theoretical and methodological approaches to the study of HCI;
- costs and benefits of incorporating an HCI perspective into the system development life cycle;
- impact of social, economic, political and cultural factors on the design of user interfaces;

Students will acquire skills in integrating HCI into the system development life cycle in:

- system analysis, including task analysis, and various information gathering methodologies, and other inputs to the design process;
- systems design and development, including I/O selection and design; graphic design; ergonomic design; dialogue, screen and error design; and tools to assist in the process (e.g., rapid prototyping tools and tools like programmable spreadsheets and database systems);
- system implementation and evaluation, including methods for implementing and testing usability of products; measurement and empirical evaluation techniques; theoretical and predictive modeling techniques, product survey methods etc.

Course Content:

The content of this course is structured around a System Development Life Cycle (SDLC). This approach recognizes the importance of different activities related to the eventual implementation of automated systems including: analysis, design, development, implementation and evaluation (Perlman, 1989; Gasen, 1987; etc.). The organization of topics from an SDLC perspective also lends itself well to the development of team projects. This perspective is on a somewhat more pragmatic level than other courses described in this report, such as CS2 (Phenomena and Theories of Human-Computer Interaction), which emphasize theory or abstraction, but may be more appropriate for students with limited exposure to the field. Recognizing that the SDLC perspective is an heuristic for organizing the material, care should be taken to ensure that students recognize and understand the iterative nature of evaluation, design, and development of interactive computing systems.

1. Introduction (N1:1, U2:4) (5 hours)

    Nature of HCI

    Application Areas

2. Analysis (U1:3, U3:1, D1:1) (5 hours)

    Market Analysis

    Feasibility Study (C/B Analysis)

    Requirements Definition (Productivity Enhancement, Product Quality Improvement, Individual Gains, Societal Gains)

    Product Acceptance Analysis

    Task Analysis

3. Design & Development (U1:1, U3:1, H1-3:4, C1-4:7, D1-2:5, D4:4) (22 hours)

    Global Design Issues (Social, Economic, and Political Factors Influencing Design)

Human Characteristics

Principles, Guidelines, & Standards

I/O Technology (Devices, Response Time, Display Rate)

Dialogue Organization (Menu, Command, Control Panel, Form Fill- in, Direct Manipulation)

Graphic Design Issues (Metaphors, Icons, Mental Maps, Representations and Presentations)

Screen Design and Layout

Language & Interaction/Error Design Issues

User Testing and Evaluation (Feasibility Labs, Prototype Construction)

User Support Development (Tutorials, On-line Help, Documentation)

Case Studies of Example Systems

4. Implementation/Evaluation (U3:1, D2:2, D3:3) (6 hours)

System Implementation Methods

Measurement and Empirical Evaluation Methods (e.g., performance and subjective measures)

Product Testing

Usability Testing (Human/Machine Fit and Adaptation)

Update and Maintenance (Nurturing the User Community)

Product Survey

5. Project Presentations and Examinations (P:4) (4 hours)

Resources:

Currently, there is no single text that encompasses the content outline described above. However, an appendix of this report describes educational resources important in designing HCI curricula, and should be helpful to individuals planning HCI courses. There are some books which might be good choices because of their breadth and/or level of technical content. Baecker & Buxton (1987) is a relatively inexpensive book containing many readings. Norman (1988) looks at the world of technology in general from a critical user's point of view. Rubinstein & Hersh (1984) focuses on designing a system from a user requirements point of view. Although there are some more recent comparable books, this one has been used successfully in several courses. Shneiderman (1987) is a survey of design and evaluation techniques for developing more usable systems. Booth (1989) is a short introduction to the field of Human-Computer Interaction that many may find useful. In addition, the curriculum module by Perlman (1989) provides a teacher with resources for creating a course in this area.

CHAPTER 4

HCI Curriculum Designs

In 1985, the ACM SIGCHI workshop on curricula in HCI (Mantei, 1985) proposed the development of courses in HCI. Since then, numerous individual courses have been developed and instituted in many parts of the world. The previous chapter has extended this work by proposing and describing an integrated set of four prototypical courses.

Some institutions, however, may wish to go further in structuring and providing HCI education for their students, and may even wish to take a leadership role in the development of entire curricula as opposed to only individual courses. The purpose of this chapter is to propose appropriate models for the design of such curricula.

We begin by suggesting one constraint that should be imposed on such designs, namely, that an HCI undergraduate curriculum generally should be embedded within an existing disciplinary curriculum rather than made to stand on its own. After listing appropriate choices for such disciplines, and discussing how such embeddings can be achieved, we propose two prototypical curricula, one in Computer Science and one in Management Information Systems. In addition we address some of the issues involved in creating an Interdisciplinary program. Examples of an HCI curriculum in Computer Science, an HCI curriculum in Information

Systems, and an Interdisciplinary HCI curriculum are described in detail in the appendices.

4.1 HCI-oriented, not HCI-centered Programs

The Curriculum Development Group feel that the adoption of a separate undergraduate degree program in HCI (major in HCI, HCI-centered program) is not now warranted. It is true that the practice of HCI entails a substantial body of knowledge, as described in Chapter 2. It is also true that HCI increasingly occupies a professional niche with a distinct identity. However, the nature of the disciplinary knowledge and the changing nature of the professional role both speak against an undergraduate program focused primarily on HCI.

Almost all the knowledge units defined in Chapter 2 lie either within or on the boundary of an established discipline. Consequently, HCI does not yet appear to have produced a unique body of knowledge which could be considered to be specific to the discipline of HCI. Furthermore, extending that existing knowledge requires a thorough grounding in the foundation areas. Finally, HCI cannot claim either a distinct research perspective or distinct research paradigm, beyond a certain uniqueness in the synthesis or dialectic of other paradigms.

While the practice of HCI can claim a certain identity, we haven't heard anyone claim that the current role is at all stable. The idea of an undergraduate degree focused exclusively on HCI therefore seems premature. At best it would be in continuing flux unbecoming a professional body. At worst it would provide a narrow training which left graduates without a base for future growth.

Nonetheless, we must also note that there are a number of students who are not well-served by the position of HCI in existing programs of study. Today's students in several disciplines typically encounter an HCI course in their senior year, if at all. At that point, a number express regret that they did not grasp the significance and appeal of HCI earlier. With most of their program complete, they are no longer able to include courses in complementary HCI disciplines. These students would like to have had the opportunity to choose an HCI orientation within their existing majors.

The CDG believes providing students the option of a set of HCI courses is both desirable and viable. An HCI orientation could inform potential students of the nature of HCI, guide their choice of supporting courses, and improve the interaction within existing HCI courses by bringing in complementary perspectives. Provided the core of existing programs is maintained, the dangers of narrow specialization can also be avoided. The remainder of this chapter contains our recommendations for curriculum developers pursuing this direction.

4.2 Base Disciplines for an HCI Orientation

We noted in Chapter 2 that HCI is an integral part of a curriculum in computing, in addition to its importance as an application and testbed area for other disciplines. Our recommendations focus on an HCI orientation within computing programs. This is not intended to speak against an HCI orientation within another discipline, such as cognitive science or human factors, or within an engineering or design school. The computing disciplines are a natural place to start, and it was there that we knew of prototypical students who had managed to put together a substantial HCI orientation within their programs of study. Finally, we focus on the computing disciplines because the CDG is a committee of a Special Interest Group of the ACM, the major professional society of the computing disciplines.

Programs with computing at their center cover a broad spectrum:

- programs whose central study is the computer itself
- programs where the central phenomenon is the process of computing and/or the computing system, including a focus on the larger "application" process of which computing is a part
- programs where the central study is some larger process, in which computing systems are a typical (but not strictly necessary) component.

Programs in electrical engineering typically incorporate the first two areas, often with an emphasis on the first area. Programs in computer science stress the second area, but may include some discussion of the first area. Programs in information systems, often developed within schools of business, information, or library science, incorporate aspects of the third area. Individual institutions may of course have programs which are broader than this minimum, and at the boundary there may appear to be little difference in the actual course content to which a student is exposed, although there may still be substantial differences in the departmental environment and perspective.

We have therefore designed frameworks for an HCI orientation within a computer science program and within a management information systems program. (Most information systems programs are called "management information systems" and are housed in a business school.) In their HCI components, these two frameworks are similar. They differ in the supporting courses which ensure the necessary overall competence in the discipline.

4.3 Adapting Existing Programs to an HCI Orientation

For an HCI orientation to be feasible, it must involve only modest change at the course level (economic feasibility) and at the program level (political feasibility). At the course level, with one or two exceptions, we have built the program framework from existing courses in existing departments. This has occasionally meant that several courses had to be included to cover the desirable HCI content, e.g., in psychology. The alternatives, new courses specifically designed for the HCI orientation, seemed unlikely to gain support in the current economic climate. Nor would they fit with the spirit of the orientation, to let each discipline speak for itself from its own paradigms.

At the program level, the inclusion of required courses in the supporting HCI disciplines implied dropping something from the existing programs. We had to choose between dropping some of the currently required courses, or eliminating some current free electives. The former choice will make it more difficult to sell the program within existing departments; the latter does not do full justice to individual differences among students and the spirit of a home-discipline based HCI orientation. As a compromise, and to make the program feasible, we have tried to do a bit of both. Thus, in the computer science framework, we recommend dropping a few required courses from typical computer science programs, some of which include a full-year of what are normally thought of as supporting mathematics courses which do not seem centrally relevant for HCI. In many computer science programs these mathematics course(s) are currently required both as a prerequisite for some computer science electives, and in the interests of general mathematical maturity.

We consider the trade-offs acceptable—to limit mathematical depth somewhat in return for depth in supporting HCI disciplines, to restrict student choice within computer science somewhat in return for a broader HCI perspective. The proposed program framework includes two specialist courses in HCI itself; we assume these would fit easily within an existing requirement of a certain number of computer science electives. We remind the reader that each proposed framework is intended as a sketch of a family of acceptable programs, and not as a single rigidly-defined program. Since course offerings within existing disciplines and beliefs about the relative importance of these offerings vary so greatly from university to university, flexibility is absolutely essential. Thus a particular institution will build on the framework according to its own identity, capabilities, student needs and faculty strengths. Examples of how this general framework can be realized or instantiated at sample institutions—not surprisingly, our own—are included in the appendices.

In part to achieve the desired flexibility, and in part to reflect a judgement of relative importance, when we list the courses within each discipline in Sections 4.4 and 4.5, we give three numbers, one corresponding to a minimum required number of courses in that discipline, one corresponding to a recommended number, and one corresponding to a maximum required number. We then present a list of typical courses in that discipline from which the desired number might to be selected in order to design a program for a particular university. We indicate our sense of the importance of these various courses by rating them in one of four ways:

- Required
- Strongly recommended
- Recommended
- A reasonable choice

Finally, our proposals assume a four year degree consisting of eight semesters in which students take five courses per semester. Individual universities with quarter systems or four courses per term can modify the proposals appropriately for their needs.

4.4 Framework for a Program Based in Computer Science

The field of HCI is not only a collection of topics spanning interaction techniques to design methodologies, cognitive models to experimental design, organizational issues to physical environments. It is fundamentally a tension between analysis and synthesis, between observation and design, between the emerging science of human-computer interaction and the poorly-understood craft of user-centered system design (Norman and Draper, 1986).

An HCI specialization within computer science can focus on training a new generation of system designers, builders, and implementers who are truly concerned with those who will ultimately use their software. We need students who are sensitive observers and incisive analysts; good conceptual thinkers and sophisticated theory builders; creative, imaginative, and elegant designers; and skilled, adept implementers. They should be familiar with a wide variety of relevant disciplines: the psychology of perception, cognitive science, software engineering, user interface management systems, graphic design, industrial design, organization theory, experimental design. They must be able to communicate with users, managers, programmers, psychologists, and graphic designers. They must have a deep commitment to and empathy with the problems of the computer user.

An HCI specialization within computer science must contain most of the contents of a good computer science degree. It must not be viewed as watered-down computer science. It must be an academic degree with a great deal of depth and rigor. We want our graduates to be able to go on to graduate work in human-computer interaction or in other areas of computer science. However, they should also be well prepared for careers in software development, interface design, or human factors either in software development companies or in corporate environments concerned with the planning, management, implementation, or use of software solutions.

More specifically, we organize the proposed curriculum in terms of four groups of courses:

- o General education (university- or faculty-wide distribution) requirements
  - Natural Science
  - Mathematics
  - Behavioral Science
  - Humanities

- o Computer science core requirements
  - Mathematics
  - Computer science

- o Requirements for the HCI specialization
  - Human-computer interaction
  - Additional computer science
  - Psychology and Cognitive Science
  - Social Science
  - Media, and Design

- o Electives

Our proposals for faculty-wide requirements and core computer science requirements are only recommendations. We believe that almost any reasonable set of faculty-wide requirements and core computer science requirements will provide an acceptable host for embedding the HCI specialization. Thus we do not insist that faculties and departments make major changes to their programs to create the specialization, although minor adjustments and a spirit of flexibility may sometimes be necessary. One example of how this could work is a description of a curriculum for a computer science specialization in "User-centered System and Interface Design" which was recently put in place by the University of Toronto Computer Science Department. That description appears in Appendix C.

In some cases, it would be advantageous for computer science students to be able to take allied field courses that are appropriate for computer science or HCI. For example, many schools offer technical writing and graphic design for engineers. Allied field courses might be offered in more than one department and not necessarily the departments in which we list them.

4.4.1 General Education Requirements

While the choice of General Education requirements is and should be at the discretion of each individual university faculty, we present below a set of recommendations that convey the flavor of our thinking. The number of such courses that we propose requiring may appear low, but this is really not the case, since each student will also be required to take a large number of courses in the behavioral sciences, the social sciences, in media, and in design, courses which achieve the effect that faculty-wide distribution requirements are intended to achieve, that is, ensuring that the student's education includes some substantive breadth.

Natural science (Terms: 2 minimum - 2 recommended - 4 maximum)

An educated professional working in the field of human-computer interaction should experience a laboratory-based science in at least one course. The student should gain some familiarity with and experience in carrying out an experiment, in collecting and analyzing data, and in developing and testing rigorous calculational and approximative models. Suitable examples are:

Physics	2 terms	Strongly recommended
Chemistry	2 terms	Recommended
Perception and Psychophysics	2 terms	Recommended

Mathematics (Terms: 2 minimum - 2 recommended - 4 maximum)

Calculus/Analysis	2 terms	Required

Behavioral Science (Terms: 2 minimum - 2 recommended - 2 maximum)

Introduction to Psychology	1-2 terms	Strongly recommended
Introduction to Sociology	1-2 terms	Strongly recommended

Humanities (Terms: 2 minimum - 2 recommended - 4 maximum)

Of critical importance is a one year course on effective writing (including some emphasis on speaking and presentation), which is a minimal attempt to address the need for effective communication in scientific and engineering disciplines. It should also make the students more skilled in the construction of documentation, help systems, error messages, and the like, and more sensitive to the importance of these aspect of systems and interfaces. An acceptable alternative is any other humanities course that will engage the student in critical thinking, organization of arguments and presentations, and expression in written (and hopefully also oral) form. First year Spanish, mathematical linguistics, microeconomics, art history, or symbolic logic are not appropriate substitutes.

Effective Writing and Speaking	2 terms	Strongly recommended
Technical Writing	2 terms	Strongly recommended
Philosophy	2 terms	Recommended
Other humanities courses (e.g., literature, political science, history)	2 terms	Recommended

4.4.2 Core Computer Science Requirements

Core computer science requirements are at the discretion of each individual department. However, our recommendations omit some of the mathematics courses which might traditionally have been required, e.g., advanced calculus and numerical analysis. In addition, some departments require one or more courses in Mathematical Statistics. This requirement has been "transformed" into a requirement for applied statistics and empirical research methodology in the behavioral sciences.

Mathematics (Terms: 1 minimum - 2 recommended - 4 maximum)

The mathematics requirements are intended to assure a minimum of mathematics literacy and sufficient competence to deal with the theoretical courses within computer science.

Discrete Math/Algebra and/or Discrete Mathematics for Computer Science	1-2 terms	Required
	1 term	Strongly recommended
Mathematical Logic	1 term	Recommended

Computer Science (Terms: 8 minimum - 8 recommended - 10 maximum)

The computer science requirements are heavy on the systems design and implementation side, a key emphasis of the program. On the other hand, we include some theoretical courses because of their importance to further study and to ensure a deep understanding of critical computer science paradigms.

The courses we list are typical of those that have been offered in Computer Science departments during the last decade. They are also fully in the spirit of what seems to have emerged from the ACM/IEEE-CS Joint Curriculum Task Force (1991), except that there is far less emphasis on hardware and computer architecture and organization.

Introduction to Computer Science	1-2 terms	Required
Computer Organization/Architecture	1 term	Required
File Structures and Data Management	1 term	Required
Programming Languages	1 term	Required
Information Structures	1 term	Required
Software Engineering	1 term	Required
Operating Systems	1 term	Strongly recommended
Automata Theory & Formal Languages	1 term	Strongly recommended
Ethics in Computer Science	1 term	Strongly recommended
Computability and Complexity	1 term	Recommended

4.4.3 Requirements for the HCI Specialization

Human-Computer Interaction (Terms: 3 minimum - 4 recommended - 5 maximum)

As proposed in Chapter 3, we recommend splitting the current typical one semester introduction to human-computer interaction into a two semester sequence, one focusing on interface design, one on HCI science. Given the growth of the field there is simply too much material for one semester without having to leave out major blocks of material. Further, the addition of a one (and preferably two) semester thesis (or a course with a large team implementation project) will guarantee that all students actually create a significant implementation and perform some observation and evaluation on what they have built. Note: The starred courses listed below are likely not in Computer Science, but in other departments.

User Interface Design and Development	1 term	Required
Phenomena and Theories of Human-Computer Interaction	1 term	Required, if available
Senior Design Project or Thesis	1-2 terms	Strongly recommended
Human Factors (*)	1 term	Recommended
Cognitive Engineering (*)	1 term	Recommended

Computer Science Electives (Terms: 1 minimum - 1 recommended - 2 maximum)

Computer Graphics	1 term	Strongly recommended
Artificial Intelligence	1 term	Strongly recommended
Information Systems Analysis & Design	1 term	Strongly recommended
Systems Engineering (*)	1 term	Recommended
Database Management/ Information Retrieval	1 term	A reasonable choice

Psychology and Cognitive Science (Terms: 3 minimum - 4 recommended - 6 maximum)

An essential aspect of our program is a behavioral science sequence, which is designed to present and integrate insights from Psychology and cognitive science. Also, we have recommended that students in this program take their statistics/research methods courses in an applied, behavioral science context. In these disciplines, statistics and experimental design are presented in a fashion that emphasizes their use in the empirical study of human behavior. Consequently, we feel the student must take either this sequence or the course on social science research methods listed below.

Introduction to Psychology	1-2 terms	Required
Statistics (Applied)	1 term	Required/strongly recommended
The Design of Experiments	1 term	Required/strongly recommended
Cognitive Psychology or Cognitive Science	1-2 terms	Required
Human Information Processing/Performance	1 term	Strongly recommended
Social Psychology	1 term	Strongly recommended

Sensation and Perception	1 term	Strongly recommended

Social Science (Terms: 3 minimum - 3 recommended - 5 maximum)

Another essential aspect of our program is a social science sequence which presents and integrates insights from organizational behavior, organization theory, sociology, and social psychology. The student must learn to appreciate the importance of and understand the dynamics of the organizational context in which technology is introduced. These courses are also becoming more important because of the increasing emphasis on systems and interfaces for computer-supported cooperative work.

Introduction to Sociology	1-2 terms	Required
Social Science Research Methods	1 term	Required/strongly recommended
Sociology of Organizations or Organizational Behavior	1 term	Strongly recommended
Social Psychology	1 term	Strongly recommended
Introduction to Ethnography	1 term	Recommended

Note: The student *must* take either the course on Social Science Research Methods or the sequence on statistics and experimental design listed under Psychology and Cognitive Science.

Media and Design (Terms: 2 minimum - 2 recommended - 4 maximum)

This final area may appear surprising to some readers, but it is essential. A key course is graphic design, particularly an information-centered, system-oriented graphic design course including the study of such topics as typography, symbolism, composition and layout, and color. Ideally, students should also do work with and gain insights from film making, video production, animation, industrial design, and sound design. They need to get practice in designing and crafting a variety of presentational artifacts since an important characteristic of an interface between humans and computers is that it is such an artifact. Although we do not expect our students to achieve professional competence in all of these media, we do expect awareness of each medium's strengths and limitations.

Graphic and/or Information Design	1 term	Required
Visual Thinking	1 term	Strongly recommended

Hypermedia/Interactive Media Design	1 term	Recommended, if available
Film Making	1 term	A reasonable choice
Video Design and Production	1 term	A reasonable choice
Animation	1 term	A reasonable choice
Industrial Design	1 term	A reasonable choice

4.4.4 Electives

(Terms: 4 minimum - 8 recommended - 12 maximum)

The choice of these elective courses is totally at the discretion of the student but ought to have some coherent rationale underlying their selection. One suggestion is that selecting credits in business or management would give the student an appreciation of the commercial world in which most software and interface work is carried out. Some relevant courses include:

Introduction to Business	1 term	A reasonable choice
Financial Accounting	1 term	A reasonable choice
Innovation and Entrepreneurship	1 term	Recommended
Software/Business Law	1 term	Recommended
Other electives.....		

Our recommended program specifies 32 out of 40 courses in general terms, allowing choice within academic disciplines in many cases, while still allowing room for eight electives totally at the student's discretion. Our minimal program specifies 28 courses, with room for 12 electives. We recommend that even a maximally intense program still allow room for four electives.

4.5 Framework for a Management Information Systems Program

This section of the report is intended to outline a curriculum which would be appropriate for individuals pursuing an HCI specialization within a business school Information Systems (IS) curriculum, typically known as Management Information Systems (MIS). It assumes that a School of Business will need to maintain its existing business core requirements, as outlined in the AACSB (American Association of Collegiate Schools of Business) accreditation standards. While this assumption limits the degree of technical specialization within a new HCI specialization, it recognizes the importance of implementing a curriculum within existing academic realities. It also helps maintain the viability of the business school, which should facilitate implementation among Schools of Business.

The primary objective is to train professionals who can create and manage information systems which are sensitive to the computer-human interface. Individuals completing this curriculum should be able to participate as members of a design team, particularly within business IS environments. They should have sufficient technical knowledge to help plan, develop, evaluate, and manage systems in such functional business areas such as marketing, financial management, operations and production, and strategic planning and management. With the knowledge of business organization and planning, they should be able to help design systems which maximize organizational, as well as HCI, goals. While technical knowledge of user interface concepts will be, of necessity, less concentrated than in a computer science major, the importance of a strong business perspective within this program should still provide an excellent complement to any design team effort.

The proposed curriculum is structured as follows:

- General education (university- or faculty-wide distribution) requirements
  - Natural science
  - Mathematics
  - Behavioral science
  - English, speech and oral communications
  - Other humanities

- Management information systems core requirements
  - Business
  - Information systems

- Requirements for the HCI specialization
  - Human-computer interaction
  - MIS or computer science
  - Psychology and cognitive science
  - Social science

o Electives

The general education, business, and information systems requirements represent a curriculum structure which incorporates the AACSB accreditation standards. The HCI area builds upon the courses and content outlined in Chapter 3 of this report.

As a result of the number of business foundation and business core courses, this proposal uses the elective portion of a typical undergraduate degree program to accommodate a specialization in HCI. In this way all traditional business and general requirements are met, but the trade-off is that very few free electives remain available to students. However, given the general nature of AACSB requirements, it may be possible to reduce or combine the number of business core requirements and still maintain both an HCI specialization and other free electives.

Finally, we must note that not all information systems programs exist within Schools of Business. Some exist within computer science environments, some in schools of information or library science, and some are independent. Each environment will impose a unique set of constraints and opportunities. To illustrate this, we include as Appendix B a description of a multidisciplinary Information Systems program in the College of Information Studies at Drexel University. This program is oriented for technical specialists rather than IS managers. Because general education and business requirements are relaxed in comparison with the program sketched below, Drexel is able to strengthen considerably the human-computer interaction, computer science, and behavioral science requirements. As with the program below, however, there is room for very few electives.

4.5.1 General Education Requirements

Natural Science (Terms: 2 minimum - 2 recommended - 2 maximum)

Physics	2 terms	A reasonable choice
Chemistry	2 terms	A reasonable choice
Biology	2 terms	A reasonable choice

Mathematics (Terms: 2 minimum - 2 recommended - 2 maximum)

College Algebra	2 terms	A reasonable choice

Introduction to Ethnography	1 term	Recommended

4.5.4 Electives

(Terms: 2 minimum - 4 recommended - 6 maximum)

Ethics in Computing	1 term	Strongly recommended
Animation	1 term	Recommended
Graphic Design	1 term	Recommended
Hypermedia	1 term	Recommended
Technical Writing	1 term	Recommended
Industrial Design	1 term	A reasonable choice

4.6 Interdisciplinary programs for HCI

The frameworks in sections 4.4 and 4.5 are intentionally multidisciplinary. Each seeks to build in-depth competence in one of the computing disciplines, supplemented by courses from other disciplines which support the study of human-computer interaction. Because the programs are built out of existing course units, there is no explicit attempt to integrate them around the HCI theme (except for the HCI courses themselves).

A truly interdisciplinary program would go beyond this coexistence of different disciplinary perspectives to both a mastery and an integration of the different disciplinary paradigms. Mastery of the paradigms would enable students to "think like" software engineers, psychologists, graphic designers, etc. so that communication with specialists from those disciplines does not flounder on conceptual or terminological differences. Integration of the paradigms requires that the program address the complementary nature of the various perspectives, either within courses or in some other explicit way. An interdisciplinary program could therefore prepare students for leadership roles within the development process for HCI - integrating the skills and knowledge of a diverse development team. (This distinction between multidisciplinary and interdisciplinary is expanded in Jantsch, 1972.)

In sections 4.4 and 4.5 we recommended frameworks for disciplinary programs oriented to HCI. One argument for the viability of the structure of those programs has been the fact that there have been a number of students who have managed to approximate the recommended course selections in their own programs (often at the cost of additional time to complete their degrees). We do not yet have such evidence for the success of a truly interdisciplinary program in HCI. Accordingly, we have not attempted to recommend a framework for an interdisciplinary program. However, the potential benefits of interdisciplinary programs seem to be so attractive that we do recommend the establishment of experimental interdisciplinary curricula which will help us learn whether such programs are feasible and what their structure should be. The structure of one such experiment, an interdisciplinary program that has been in existence at the University of Guelph since the fall of 1989, is outlined in Appendix D.

In the remainder of this section we describe why we believe such experiments are worthwhile, i.e., how an interdisciplinary program might be a valuable addition to programs following the frameworks of the previous sections. Students who seek to combine the study of two disciplines can often do so now by opting for a joint major, offering a selection of courses in the two areas. This could be accomplished with an HCI focus by majoring in Computer Science and Psychology, for example. There are two limitations with this approach. First, it will not provide support for the integration of the two disciplines, as outlined above. In addition, because of the breadth requirements within each of the twin majors, it will be difficult to go beyond the two major subjects to include other areas of importance for HCI.

Ideally, an HCI specialist would be equally comfortable dealing with technological issues, the needs of individuals and the concerns of their organizations and workgroups. We know of individual HCI practitioners who have achieved a substantial competence along these lines, but they often express dissatisfaction at their own lack of fundamental groundings outside the discipline they have studied formally. Therefore, we recommend that an interdisciplinary HCI curriculum should develop a sense of mastery in:

- the technological perspective of computing
- the ergonomics issues at an individual level, from cognitive science or human factors curricula
- the "system" issues, from disciplines like organizational science, information systems, or sociology.

This mastery is necessary for political as well as professional reasons. We want the students in HCI to be respected by faculty from other disciplines (partly to insure that the study of HCI is also respected). The program would have to include depth within each discipline, although the breadth may be limited to areas directly supporting HCI.

What about all the other areas which are pertinent to designing effective user interfaces: graphic design, physical ergonomics, technical writing, education and training? Given that no program can cover everything, these will probably have to be treated in a cursory way through isolated electives. HCI students could come to appreciate the importance of these areas and master specific HCI-relevant skills, but will not be required to achieve broad competence.

These recommendations are deliberately somewhat speculative. Until we have more evidence from experimental programs, we will not know how successfully the various disciplines can cooperate to offer such an interdisciplinary program. But the clarity of the need for interdisciplinary approaches in HCI provides excellent motivation for both faculty and students.

CHAPTER 5

Issues Raised By Our Recommendations

There are three classes of issues raised by this report: issues concerned with how to implement our recommendations, issues that remain unresolved, and limitations of our recommendations. Wanting to complete the report before the end of this millennium we did not attempt to detail the various ways in which organizations or universities might use our findings. We have also deliberately not addressed certain issues. These issues are mentioned in this section of the report to assure readers that we were aware of them when compiling this report. Finally, we would like to encourage others to treat the proposals contained in this report as being subject to change and encourage them to take up where we left off.

5.1 Implementation Suggestions

Often reports are written which seldom see utilization beyond their initial dissemination. We are particularly interested in seeing this report discussed, debated and used as much as possible by the broadest range of individuals with an interest in HCI. In order to facilitate its use, we offer the following specific suggestions concerning this report's use and the implementation of its recommendations.

5.1.1 As a Self-Assessment Tool

One of the ways in which this report could be used is to assist in an individual's self assessment in HCI. Specifically, we can envision students, faculty, and professionals using it to assess their own strengths and weaknesses with respect to the content of the field. Students could use the report in a number of additional ways. For example, the content outline might be used to help them assess their level of career preparation at the end of their studies. Or, the report might be used to help a student select a university program which offers preparation in HCI. Certainly, we would hope that faculty will use the report to assist them in designing individual HCI courses and curricula. This report might also help groups of faculty to cooperatively review curricula as an aid in designing specializations within an interdisciplinary HCI focus. Non-academic professionals should also find the report helpful. For example, this report might well be used to help pinpoint pertinent areas for in-house training or continuing education in the form of tutorials or short courses.

5.1.2 As a Resource Guide

While this entire report could be viewed as a resource, the articulation of content areas (Chapter 2) and the listing of resources (Appendix A) should be particularly useful for a variety of applications. For example, the overview of content areas should be helpful in designing new or revised courses which extend beyond those currently offered or those presented in this report. The annotated resource guide should be useful in pointing individuals to a variety of information sources on relevant topics in HCI, for purposes of research, teaching or continuing education.

5.1.3 As a Rationale for Institution-Specific Recommendations

Any new course or curriculum recommendation should be supported by documentation which includes the rationale for the effort. We intend that this report provide some of the supporting rationale and initial structure necessary for developing institution-specific recommendations within HCI. This type of information would be most helpful to faculty and administrators developing HCI courses or curricula within their respective institutions. It is assumed that this report can be viewed as a guide to program development, subject to modification based upon the specific requirements and situations present within each institution. One goal of the report has been to provide enough structural flexibility to make such adaptation possible.

5.1.4 As an Impetus for Continuing Education

Given the rapidly changing nature of HCI, the importance of keeping up to date within the field is an ongoing challenge. We hope that this report would be used to help assess and structure continuing education possibilities for faculty and professionals who are focusing within HCI. Both formal and informal methods of acquiring additional knowledge and skill within HCI could be structured by using the content areas within this report as a guide. We are particularly interested in encouraging innovative approaches to continuing education through exchanges of faculty and non-academic professionals between higher education research labs and centers and industry. In a field such as HCI, hands-on experience is critical to the development of skills, but the opportunity to reflect upon what one has done, why, and how well it worked is also critical. The HCI specialty of Computer Supported Cooperative Work (CSCW) might, for example, be used as a vehicle to create, share and develop continuing education possibilities between academia and industry.

5.2 Unresolved Issues

A number of issues were left unresolved by our committee. This is not to say that we were uninterested in resolving them. We had to stop someplace. For example, we did not design courses for either the graduate level work or for continuing education. We did not design an independent HCI curriculum (although there are some initial attempts at such a curriculum described within this report and its appendices). We did not design courses or a curriculum for a school of design (although an increasing number of such schools are developing an interest in design issues in HCI). Nor did we grapple with identifying and delimiting the market for either the field or its students. Finally, we did not attempt to spell out specific careers paths which students of HCI might follow.

5.2.1 Graduate and Continuing Education Courses

The course and curriculum issues discussed in this report are focused on undergraduate instruction. We have not tried to design a graduate program. However, at this stage in our thinking it seems that the mapping of the content areas into courses at the graduate level could be done in several ways, one of which includes up to five or six courses on the major topics, as broken down in our analysis in Chapter 3. Furthermore, based on discussions with several of our colleagues we are encouraged to believe that there exists at some institutions great potential for a truly interdisciplinary post graduate program in HCI which crosses departmental and even collegial boundaries.

We have also not tried to design courses for those working in a non-academic environment. We are confident, however, that those concerned with industrial training will be able to make use of the report as it is structured. Given our analysis of the content of the field and the mapping of that content into example courses, other course designers should be able to create an appropriate mapping of content into the design of short courses suitable for their own audiences. As mentioned above, the content description provides a framework against which to assess needed courses, the resource material should help the short-course designer find sources for course content, and the example courses can serve as models for still other courses with slightly different foci.

5.2.2 Curriculum

Only after attempting to design a curriculum can one fully appreciate the scope of the task involved. The CDG started out with the goal of developing an entire HCI curriculum—from Bachelor's Degree to Ph.D.—and ended up specifying four courses and two sample undergraduate curricula. Part of the complexity of curriculum design in this case arises from the relationship of HCI to many different disciplines, which suggests that an HCI curriculum could be housed comfortably in a number of different departments, e.g., Computer Science, Psychology, Information Systems, or Industrial Engineering. Furthermore, the boundaries of the HCI discipline are still fairly dynamic, as evidenced by recent emphasis upon computer-supported cooperative work with the necessary incorporation of pertinent social psychological and sociological theory. In summary, one of the tasks left undone by this group is the specification of how HCI relates to various established disciplines. We currently feel strongly that HCI appears by nature to be multidisciplinary and would hope, as HCI develops further, that it does not get absorbed into a single discipline. The study of HCI and its intimate relationship to a rapidly changing technology seems to require multiple points of view as a way of avoiding an overly narrow focus.

Being multidisciplinary also makes it difficult for HCI to be piggybacked onto existing model curricula, such as the Report of the ACM Task Force on the Core of Computer Science (Denning, *et al.*, 1988). Certain content areas appropriate to HCI would surely suffer by constricting HCI entirely into a subarea of Computer Science, as seems to be recommended by the Denning report. On the other hand, there is a benefit to expanding upon such a vehicle as a computer science curriculum. Such expansion would make accreditation of an HCI program possible by housing it in a larger curriculum which is accreditable by the Computer Sciences Accreditation Board. As a result of the multidisciplinary content of HCI it seems probable that a similar case can be made for housing an HCI curriculum in any traditional discipline, accreditable or not. Currently, however, it seems that housing a full fledged HCI curriculum within an AACSB (American Association of Collegiate Schools of Business) accredited business school Information Systems program would be a difficult task as it appears that the need to include several different content areas would suffer and threaten AACSB accreditation. Therefore, our group has avoided specification of where HCI would best reside, leaving this up to implementers of individual programs.

5.2.3 Market

An important issue of concern to university program administrators that has also been left out of consideration by this group concerns the market aspects of an HCI curriculum. For instance, this group did not consider issues of how many interested and available students there might be for HCI, both now and in the future; of how many jobs for those students might exist upon graduation; or of how many programs might be interested in incorporating our recommendations. Such estimations would have to be based on an assessment of the need for HCI education and projections for its growth over the next decade or so. Given our time and resource limitations, this group simply did not take these questions under consideration and leaves them for program administrators to evaluate for themselves. (However, as one might suspect, our best guess is that there will be growth in the need for graduates with the skills and knowledge provided by education in HCI.)

5.2.4 Careers

An additional issue closely related to marketing any new program or curriculum is that of potential career paths for graduates. This group did not address this issue which would involve generation of job descriptions and a skills inventory. HCI is so new and so rapidly changing that a skills inventory would be premature and obsolete as soon as it was published. As the discipline matures and stabilizes, a common set of exit skills and jobs for which those skills are used could be developed.

5.3 Known Limitations

5.3.1 Implementation Limitations

While this group did discuss issues of curriculum implementation, and many of them are mentioned in this chapter, general administrative aspects of curriculum implementation were not addressed, such as sources of program or faculty development funding. In addition, pathways for piecewise incorporation of HCI courses into different existing curricula were not described. The circumstances and details of individual programs and their administration make such recommendations on the part of this group inappropriate at this time. Furthermore, we trust to the creativity and imagination of our fellow educators in developing proposals for institution-specific recommendations to their own administrative decision makers.

5.3.2 Group Representativeness

We should also address the limitations of our recommendations in terms of the small size of our group and the representativeness or non-representativeness of its membership. While we feel comfortable with the definitions, content coverage and recommendations made, this was a relatively small group which did not represent all of the HCI-related disciplines. Although we tried to counter this limitation through the creation of a Curriculum Advisory Panel which was more broadly representative there are still limitations to the representativeness of this report, some of which we are aware and some of which neither our Advisory Panel nor our many volunteer reviewers have caught or addressed. One example of an area not explicitly represented in this report is the ongoing work on user interfaces in the artificial intelligence community. The interested reader should consult Sullivan and Tyler (1991) for a sample of the type of work currently going on in that area. Another example of a fruitful line of development in work on user interfaces not adequately represented in this report involves the relationships among the film, video, and graphic design disciplines and HCI, areas of emerging importance to the field.

5.3.3 Model of the Development Process

Finally, the picture of the interface development process as described in some places in this report may seem rooted in the waterfall model of software development. Some of that impression comes from the organizational structure imposed on the report, some of it comes from our not having taken more careful pains to structure the report so as to avoid that impression. However, if one believes in the process of iterative design and prototyping, then the design-implement-evaluate sequence--viewed as a rigid and inflexible series of steps, each one of which is to be completed before proceeding to the next--no longer makes a great deal of sense, and promotes an unnecessarily limited view of design and evaluation. As argued by several authors (e.g., Gould and Lewis, 1985; Hewett, 1986; Norman, 1988) the first step in good design is evaluation and understanding of existing tools and practices in the existing task and work environment. This is especially true when existing practice is more and more likely to include computer use. Also, empirical evaluation of prototypes using real users is a key part of prototyping and iterative design. After-the-implementation evaluation is a practice of "too little, too late" which should be avoided.

5.4 Conclusion

In conclusion, we hope that this report will be useful to a variety of individuals with several different goals and intended applications. Both the report as a whole and our recommendations are meant to be taken in the spirit of a stimulus for further discussion and for eventual revision. If we have created a useful structure and some interest in furthering the field of HCI, especially in its promotion within the university community, then we will have accomplished our goal.

References

ACM Curriculum Committee on Computer Science. (1968). Curriculum 68: Recommendations for academic programs in computer science. *Communications of the ACM, 11*, 3 (March), 151-197.

ACM Curriculum Committee on Computer Science. (1977). Curriculum recommendations for the undergraduate program in computer science. *SIGCSE Bulletin* (ACM), 2 (June), 1-16.

ACM Curriculum Committee on Computer Science. (1979). Curriculum 78: Recommendations for the undergraduate program in computer science. *Communications of the ACM, 22*, 3 (March), 147-166.

ACM/IEEE-CS Joint Curriculum Task Force. (1991). *Computing Curricula 1991*, ACM Baltimore, MD. (Order No. 201880)

Baecker, R. and Buxton, W. (1987). *Readings in Human-Computer Interaction*. Los Altos, CA: Morgan Kaufmann.

Denning, P. J., *et al*. (1988). *Report on the ACM Task Force on the Core of Computer Science*. New York: ACM Press (Order No. 201880).

Englebart, D. C. (1963). A conceptual framework for the augmentation of man's intellect. In Howerton and Weeks (Eds.) *Vistas in Information Handling*, Vol. 1. (pp. 1-29) Washington, DC: Spartan Books.

Gasen, J. G. (1987). Human factors design in information systems: Curriculum and teaching issues. In *Proceedings of Information Systems Education Conference*, San Francisco, CA.

Gould, J. D. and Lewis, C. (1985). Designing for usability: Key principles and what designers think. *Communications of the ACM, 28*, 300-311.

Green, P. (1984). Teaching a course on human factors and computer systems. *IEEE Computer Graphics and Applications, 4* (12), 43-45.

Helander, Martin (1989). *Handbook of Human-Computer Interaction*. Amsterdam: North-Holland.

Hewett, T. T. (1987a). An undergraduate course in software psychology. *ACM SIGCHI Bulletin, 18* (3), 43-49.

Hewett, T. T. (1987b). The computer as a tool in instructional computing: Students as software architects. *Behavior Research Methods, Instruments & Computers, 19*, 123-127.

Hewett, T. T. (1986). The role of iterative evaluation in designing systems for usability. In M. D. Harrison and A. F. Monk (Eds.), *People and Computers: Designing for Usability* (pp. 196-214). Cambridge: Cambridge University Press.

Hix, D. (1990). Teaching a course in human-computer interaction. *Computer Science Education, 1*(3), 253-268.

IEEE Computer Society Education Committee/Model Curriculum Subcommittee. (1976). *A Curriculum in computer science and engineering*. IEEE Computer Society, Committee Report.

IEEE Computer Society Educational Activities Board/Model Program Committee. (1983). The 1983 IEEE Computer Society model program in computer science and engineering. *IEEE Computer Society*, December.

Jantsch, E. (1972). Inter- and transdisciplinary University: A systems approach to education and innovation, *Higher Education, 1*, 7-37.

Kantowitz, B. H. and Sorkin, R. D. (1983). *Human Factors: Understanding People-System Relationships*. New York: John Wiley & Sons.

Kay, A. and Goldberg, A. (1977). Personal dynamic media. *IEEE Computer, 10* (3), 31-42.

Licklider, J. C. R. (1960). Man-computer symbiosis. *IRE Transactions on Human Factors in Electronics, HFE-1* (1), 4-11.

Lindsay, P. H. and Norman, D. A. (1977). *Human Information Processing*. (2nd ed.). New York: Academic Press.

Mantei, M. M. (1985). Recommendations of the SIGCHI curriculum workshop. *ACM SIGCHI Bulletin, 17* (2), 17-19.

Newell, A., Perlis, A. & Simon, H. (1967). What is computer science? *Science, 157*, 1373-4.

Newman, W. and Sproull, R. (1972). *Principles of Computer Graphics*. Englewood Cliffs, NJ: Prentice-Hall.

Norman, D. A. (1988). *The Psychology of Everyday Things*. New York: Basic Books. (Reissued in 1989 as *The Design of Everyday Things*. New York: Doubleday.)

Norman, D. A. and Draper, S. W. (Eds.). (1986). *User Centered System Design: New Perspectives on Human-Computer Interaction*. Hillsdale, NJ: Erlbaum.

Nunamaker, J. F., Jr., Couger, J. D. & Davis, G. B. (Eds.) (1982). Information systems curriculum recommendations for the 80s: Undergraduate and graduate programs, a report of the ACM Curriculum Committee on Information Systems. *Communications of the ACM, 25*, 781-805.

Perlman, G. (1989). *User Interface Development: Curriculum Module SEI-CM-17-1.1*, Second Edition. Pittsburgh, PA: Carnegie-Mellon University Software Engineering Institute.

Rubinstein, R. and Hersh, H. (1984). *The Human Factor: Designing Computer Systems for People*. Burlington, Mass.: Digital Press.

Salvendy, G. (1987). *Handbook of Human Factors*. New York: John Wiley & Sons.

Sanders, M.S. and McCormick, E.J. (1987). *Human Factors in Engineering and Design*. Sixth Edition, New York: McGraw-Hill.

Shaw, M. (ed.) (1985). *The Carnegie-Mellon Curriculum for Undergraduate Computer Science*. New York: Springer Verlag.

Shneiderman, B. (1987). *Designing the User Interface: Strategies for Effective Human-Computer Interaction*. Reading, MA: Addison-Wesley.

Strong, G. W. (1989). Introductory course in human computer interaction. *ACM SIGCHI Bulletin, 20* (3), 19-21.

Suchman, L. (1987). *Plans and Situated Actions: The Problem of Human Machine Communication*. Cambridge: Cambridge University Press.

Sullivan, J. W. and Tyler, S. W. (Eds.) (1991). *Intelligent User Interfaces*. New York: ACM Press (Addison-Wesley).

Sutherland, I. (1963). Sketchpad: A man-machine graphical communication system. *AFIPS Spring Joint Computer Conference, 23*, 329-346.

Verplank, B. and Kim, S. (1987). Graphic invention for user interfaces: An experimental course in user-interface design. *ACM SIGCHI Bulletin, 18* (3), 50-66.

APPENDIX A

Resources for Human-Computer Interaction

Readers of this report, especially those who are just entering the field, may find it helpful to refer to a list of basic resources introducing the field of Human Computer Interaction. We can suggest as a starting point some books, papers, videotapes, journals, periodicals, and conferences. (These lists have been adapted and modified from Baecker and Buxton, 1987, with assistance from materials provided by Gary Perlman and Ben Shneiderman.)

A.1 Books

Four books that present general, highly readable introductions to principles of effective user interface design are Rubinstein and Hersh (1984), Shneiderman (1987), Heckel (1982), and Gaines and Shaw (1984). Booth (1989) is a good introduction to human-computer interaction. Nickerson (1986) is an articulate review of many aspects of human-computer interaction in the context of how computers are applied and used. Bolt (1984) gives a sense of how our interactions with computers may eventually be qualitatively different from what they are now. Laurel (1990) is a lively and stimulating collection of essays on the art of human-computer interface design. Norman (1988) is an inspirational and thought-provoking discussion of design that shows us how we can learn about good and bad design just by observing the strengths and weaknesses of the everyday things we find throughout the world. Greenbaum and Kyng (1991) is the most accessible introduction to cooperative, or participatory, design.

At an intermediate level, Baecker and Buxton (1987) is a good place to begin, as it contains 60 classic papers or excerpts of books integrated with 20 original essays that together provide a deep, comprehensive view of the field of human-computer interaction. (Sometime during 1992 this collection will be replaced by a new edition with an additional editor. The bridging essays will include 25-50% new material and 75-80% of the readings will be new.) Helander (1988) is an advanced and comprehensive collection of essays on the field of human-computer interaction.

A number of valuable books deal with more specialized topics. Perlman (1989a) contains a detailed annotated outline on the design, implementation, and evaluation of user interface software, It is intended to help teachers design courses, and also contains a set of support materials to help teach courses. Curtis (1985) contains numerous valuable papers on human factors in software development. Card, Moran, and Newell (1983) is a comprehensive and deep introduction to one family of models of the human user of computer systems. Norman and Draper (1986) and Carroll (1987) are two useful references for those wanting to think more deeply about the cognitive aspects of human-computer interaction.

Nielsen (1990) is a readable introduction to hypertext. Grief (1987) and Galegher, Kraut, and Egido (1990) provide valuable introductions to the field of computer-supported cooperative work. Sauter, Chapman, and Knutson (1986) survey and recommend solutions to many of the health concerns that have developed around the use of VDT's. Westin, Schweder, Baker, and Lehman (1985) provide a guide to managing the people, organizational, and regulatory aspects of office technology.

It may also be helpful to refer to classic texts on human factors such as Sanders and McCormick (1987). Salvendy (1987) is a comprehensive handbook of human factors. Smith and Mosier (1986) is one of the most detailed lists of guidelines for designing user interface software. Apple (1987) presents a valuable example of a set of guidelines specific to a particular desktop interface style. Ray and Ravizza (1985) is a valuable introduction to the methods of behavioral observation and experimentation for those with little background in the area. Other useful sources on empirical evaluation are Campbell and Stanley (1963) and Hewett (1986).

A.2 Papers

An extremely valuable resource is the HCI Bibliography described in Perlman (1991). This resource is an on-line bibliography of much of the literature of HCI that is available through network and electronic mail access, and Mac and DOS floppy disks. Three papers that discuss the teaching of user interface development are Perlman (1989b, 1990a, 1990b).

A.3 Videotapes

Increasingly, videotapes are being used to present the dynamic, interactive nature of modern user interfaces. Videotapes submitted to the ACM SIGCHI Conferences are often published in the ACM SIGGRAPH Video Review (1983-present). Other valuable videotapes based on short courses organized by Ben Shneiderman are published by the University of Maryland (1987-present).

A.4 Journals and Periodicals

The major journals reporting results on human-computer interaction are the *International Journal of Man-Machine Studies* (1969-present), *Behaviour and Information Technology* (1983-present), *Human-Computer Interaction* (1983-present), *Interacting with Computers* (1989-present), the *International Journal on Human Computer Interaction* (1989-present), *ACM Transactions on Information Systems* (1983-present), and *Human Factors* (1959-present). Another useful regular source of information is the *ACM SIGCHI Bulletin* (1982-present).

A.5 Conferences

The major conferences at which recent results are presented and published are the annual ACM CHI conference (1983-present), the IFIP INTERACT conference (1984-present), the British Computer Society HCI conference (1985-present), the International Conference on Human-Computer Interaction (1985-present), and the annual meeting of the Human Factors Society (1957-present). Other more specialized but relevant conferences include the annual conference on User Interface Software and Technology (1988-present), the biennual Hypertext Conference (1987-present), and the biennual Conference on Computer Supported Cooperative Work (1986-present).

A.6 References

Apple Computer (1987). *Human Interface Guidelines: The Apple Desktop Interface*. Reading, MA.: Addison-Wesley Publishing Company.

Baecker, R. M. and Buxton, W. A. S. (1987). *Readings in Human-Computer Interaction*. San Mateo CA.: Morgan Kaufmann Publishers. (This book under revision.)

Behaviour and Information Technology (1982-present). Published quarterly by Taylor & Francis, Inc., 242 Cherry Street, Philadelphia Pennsylvania 19106 USA.

Bolt, R.A. (1984). *The Human Interface: Where People and Computers Meet*. Boston: Lifetime Learning Publications.

Booth, P. (1989). *An Introduction to Human-Computer Interaction*. Hillsdale, N.J.: Lawrence Erlbaum Associates.

Campbell, D., and Stanley, J. (1963). *Experimental and Quasi-experimental Designs for Research*. Chicago: Rand-McNally.

Card, S. K., Moran, T. P., & Newell, A. (1983). *The Psychology of Human-Computer Interaction*. Hillsdale, N.J.: Lawrence Erlbaum Associates.

Carroll, J. (Ed.). (1987). *Interfacing Thought: Cognitive Aspects of Human-Computer Interaction*. Cambridge, MA.: MIT Press.

CHI Conference (1982-present). The annual Conference on Human Factors in Computing Systems is sponsored by the Special Interest Group on Computers and Human Interaction (SIGCHI) of the Association for Computing Machinery (ACM), 1515 Broadway, New York, N.Y., 10036. The Proceedings are published by ACM Press and have also been distributed by Addison-Wesley Publishing Company. Through CHI'90, the Proceedings were a special issue of the *SIGCHI Bulletin*.

Computer Supported Cooperative Work Conference (1986-present). The Proceedings of this biennual conference are published by ACM.

Curtis, B. (1985). *Tutorial: Human Factors in Software Development*. Second Edition. Washington, DC: IEEE Computer Society Press.

Galegher, J., Kraut, R. E., and Egido, C. (1990). *Intellectual Teamwork: Social and Technological Foundations of Cooperative Work*. Hillsdale, N.J.: Lawrence Erlbaum Associates.

Greenbaum, J. and Kyng, M. (1991). *Design at Work: Cooperative Design of Computer Systems*. Hillsdale, N.J.: Lawrence Erlbaum Associates.

Greif, I. (Ed.) (1987). *Computer-Supported Cooperative Work: A Book of Readings*. San Mateo CA.: Morgan Kaufmann Publishers.

HCI Conference (1985-present). The annual conference on People and Computers is sponsored primarily by the British Computer Society. Proceedings of these conferences are regularly published by Cambridge University Press as part of its "People and Computers" series.

Heckel, P. (1982). *The Elements of Friendly Software Design*. New York: Warner Books.

Helander, M. (1988). *Handbook of Human-Computer Interaction*. Amsterdam: North-Holland.

Hewett, T. T. (1986). The role of iterative evaluation in designing systems for usability. In M. D. Harrison and A. F. Monk (Eds.), *People and Computers: Designing for Usability* (pp. 196-214). Cambridge: Cambridge University Press.

Human Computer Interaction (1985-present). Published quarterly by Lawrence Erlbaum Associates, Inc., 365 Broadway, Hillsdale New Jersey 07642 USA.

Human Factors (1959-present). Published bimonthly by The Human Factors Society, Inc., P.O.Box 1369, Santa Monica California 90406 USA.

Human Factors Society Annual Meeting (1957-present). The proceedings are published by The Human Factors Society, Inc., P.O.Box 1369, Santa Monica California 90406 USA.

Hypertext Conference (1987-present). The Proceedings of this biennual conference are published by ACM.

Interact Conference (1984-present). The IFIP conference on Human-Computer Interaction is sponsored primarily by the International Federation of Information Processing (TC 13). The most recent meeting was held from August 27 through 31, 1990, in Cambridge, England, in conjunction with the British Computer Society. The proceedings are published by North-Holland.

Interacting with Computers (1989-present). Published triannually by Butterworth Scientific Ltd., P) Box 63, Westbury House, Bury Street, Guildford, Surrey, GU2 5BH, UK.

International Conference on Human-Computer Interaction (1985-present). This conference is sponsored by the International Commission on Human Aspects of Computing, Geneva, Switzerland. The most recent meeting was held from September 18 through 22, 1989, in Boston, Massachusetts. The proceedings are published by Elsevier.

International Journal of Man-Machine Studies (1969-present). Published monthly by Academic Press Inc. (London) Limited, High Street, Foots Cray, Sidcup Kent DA14 5HP England.

International Journal on Human Computer Interaction (1989-present). Published quarterly by Ablex Publishing Company, 355 Chestnut Street, Norwood NJ 07648 USA.

Laurel, B. (1990). *The Art of Human-Computer Interface Design*. Reading, Mass.: Addison-Wesley Publishing Company.

Marca, D. and Bock, G. *Groupware: Software for Computer Supported Cooperative Work*. Los Alamitos, CA; IEEE Computer Society Press.

Marcus, A. (1991). *Graphic Design for Electronic Documents and User Interfaces*. Reading, MA: Addison-Wesley.

Nickerson, R. S. (1986). *Using Computers: Human Factors in Information Systems*. Cambridge, Mass.: MIT Press.

Nielsen, J. (1990). *Hypertext and Hypermedia*. Boston, MA.: Academic Press, Inc.

Norman, D.A. (1988). *The Psychology of Everyday Things*. New York: Basic Books, Inc. (in paper (1990). *The Design of Everyday Things*. New York: Doubleday)

Norman, D.A. and Draper, S.W. (Eds.), (1986). *User Centered System Design: New Perspectives on Human-Computer Interaction*. Hillsdale, N.J.: Lawrence Erlbaum Associates.

Perlman, G. (1989a). *User Interface Development Curriculum Module*. Available from the Director of Education, Software Engineering Institute, Carnegie-Mellon University, Pittsburgh PA 15213.

Perlman, G. (1989b). Teaching User Interface Development to Software Engineers, *Proceedings of the Human Factors Society - 32nd Annual Meeting*, pp. 391-394.

Perlman, G. (1990a). Teaching User Interface Development, *IEEE Software*, 7(6), pp. 85-86.

Perlman, G. (1990b). Teaching User Interface Development to Software Engineering and Computer Science Majors, *ACM SIGCHI Bulletin*, 22(1), pp. 61-66.

Perlman, G. (1991). The HCI Bibliography Project, *ACM SIGCHI Bulletin*, 23(3), pp. 15-20.

Ray, W. J. and Ravizza, R. (1986). *Methods Toward a Science of Behavior and Experience*. Second Edition, Belmont, CA.: Wadsworth Publishing Company.

Rubinstein, R. and Hersh, H. (1984). *The Human Factor: Designing Computer Systems for People*. Burlington, Mass.: Digital Press.

Salvendy, G. (1987). *Handbook of Human Factors*. New York: John Wiley & Sons.

Sanders, M.S. and McCormick, E.J. (1987). *Human Factors in Engineering and Design*. Sixth Edition, New York: McGraw-Hill.

Sauter, S. L., Chapman, L. J. & Knutson, S. J. (1985). *Improving VDT Work: Causes and Control of Health Concerns in VDT Use*. Madison: University of Wisconsin. (Distributed by The Report Store, 910 Massachusetts St., Suite 503, Lawrence Kansas 66044 USA.)

Shneiderman, B. (1986). *Designing the User Interface: Strategies for Human-Computer Interaction*. Reading, Mass.: Addison-Wesley Publishing Company.

SIGCHI Bulletin (1982-present). This quarterly is published by the Special Interest Group on Computers and Human Interaction (SIGCHI) of the Association for Computing Machinery (ACM), 11 W. 42nd Street, New York, N.Y., 10036.

SIGGRAPH Video Review (1983-present). A catalog describing these video publications is available from the ACM. Many have sections pertinent to HCI.

Smith, S. L. and Mosier, J. N. (1986). *Guidelines for Designing User Interface Software*. Report ESD-TR-86-278, The MITRE Corporation, Bedford MA 01730. (Available from National Technical Information Service, Springfield, VA.)

Transactions on Information Systems (1983-present). Published quarterly by the ACM, ibid.

University of Maryland Instructional Television (1987-present). Videotapes of Ben Shneiderman's HCI short courses, College Park, MD.

User Interface Software Technology Conference (1988-present). The proceedings of this annual conference are published by ACM.

Westin, A., Schweder, H., Baker, M. & Lehman, S. (1985). *The Changing Workplace: A Guide to Managing the People, Organizational and Regulatory Aspects of Office Technology.* White Plains, NY: Knowledge Industry Publications, Inc.

APPENDIX B

An Information Systems Curriculum in Human-Computer Interaction

Gary Strong
College of Information Studies
Drexel University

B.1 Introduction

This is a proposal for an undergraduate CHI concentration in an interdisciplinary undergraduate information systems curriculum. The basis for this proposal is an existing undergraduate degree in Information Systems at Drexel University which has received international attention as an innovative program in a novel setting.[1] The State of Pennsylvania recently approved the designation of Drexel's degree as a BSIS Degree (Bachelors of Science in Information Systems). While most information systems programs are taught within Business Schools or Computer Science Departments, this program is housed in an interdisciplinary college that has no departments. It is, therefore, experimental. The program has been in existence since 1984 and appears to be highly successful as measured by the salaries and satisfaction level of graduates and the wages paid to co-op students during their studies. It seems that this program has CHI, in its most general context, as its main philosophy since the program was specifically

1. Strong, G.W.; Woodward, D. & Dehdashti-Jones, P. (1987). An Information Systems Curriculum: An American Experiment. In: R.A. Buckingham, R.A. Hirschheim, F.F. Land & C.J. Tully. (eds.), *Information Systems Education: Recommendations and Implementation*. Cambridge: Cambridge University Press, pp. 204-214

designed to train students who could produce information systems that emphasize the human component of systems.

The purpose of this paper is to present a concentration in CHI within the context of a generalized version of Drexel's information systems curriculum, taking into account that most readers are familiar with four-year, semester-based programs. Drexel classes are term-based, meaning that they are 10 weeks long, and there are four terms per year. Furthermore, students attend for five years, and after their Freshman year, students attend during the Summer term, as in any other term. The program length results from the fact that Drexel is a cooperative education university. Most students are employed for 6 months in each of the three middle years of their five-year program. Such a program produces students who are highly-valued by employers due to the experience gained during co-op. Furthermore, the co-op experience brings an added dimension to the classroom, in that it serves as a real-life laboratory for students to practice their skills and to have a chance to return to their professors with questions and discoveries from such experience. Later classroom learning is enriched by co-op experience and can proceed at a more mature level with students who are driven by issues from real-life projects.

B.2 Objectives

The objective of the overall BSIS program is to train professionals who can create information systems that both achieve organizational objectives, such as competitive advantage, and augment human work in a natural and productive way. The objective of a specific concentration in CHI within the information systems program is to generate students who participate in the development of systems by specializing in the design and evaluation of computer-human interfaces. This is no small task since information technology has a radical and ever-changing impact upon organizational infrastructure in terms of the way people communicate, carry on their work, and manage each other. In addition, the concept of an interface has recently been generalized beyond being identified with a one human/one computer channel to include multiple, complex relationships between humans and computers as components of larger information systems. Understanding how tasks and knowledge can be shared in a natural fashion between humans and computers to accomplish organizational goals is a major contribution that students of this concentration can provide. They will be able to "engineer" information architectures by assembling into systems semi-autonomous functional modules, be they human or computer, to accomplish specific organizational goals. The term "engineer" is used purposefully here in agreement with an article that claims that engineering rather than computer science is the proper disciplinary domain of information systems professionals due to the applied nature of the work.[2]

B.3 Prerequisites

Entering freshmen in information systems are expected to have an interest in science and mathematics to insure success with the technical aspects of the program, but they must also have an overriding concern for human behavior and its intricate relationship with technology. Although the program is highly technical, it is not a "techy" degree. Most students who have succeeded in it at Drexel performed equally well in both math and verbal SAT's and were looking for a career that balances computer science with humanistic studies.

B.4 Course Requirements

The proposed course requirements for a BSIS with a concentration in CHI are shown below, categorized into topic areas that may be serviced by different university departments. It has been assumed that there are 40 semester courses in the 4-year program structure. In the list of semester courses which follows, courses specific to the CHI Concentration in IS are indicated with an asterisk. Such courses would be different for IS students who are not concentrating in CHI, such as those students in the other concentrations at Drexel (Distributed Systems, Information Resource Management, and Systems Analysis and Design). Where appropriate, topics related to CHI but covered in non-CHI concentration courses are indicated below with the course names prefixed by "Includes ...".

2. Lewis, P.M. (September 1989). Information Systems is an Engineering Discipline. *Communications of the ACM, 32*, pp. 1045-7

I. Information Systems (12 courses)

1. Introduction to Information Systems
   - Includes a lab on the use of computer applications
   - Includes capabilities and limitations of computer hardware

2.&3. Systems Analysis I & II
   - Includes development of user requirements
   - Includes life-cycle and prototyping methodologies
   - Includes joint application development sessions and walkthroughs
   - Includes quality assurance techniques

4.&5. Database I & II
   - Includes user views

6. Information Resource Management

7. Data Communication and Networking
   - Includes Open-System Interconnection model

8. Introduction to Human-Computer Interaction (Required in all concentrations)

9. User Interface Design

10. Evaluation of User Interfaces

11. Computer-Supported Cooperative Work

12. Senior Design Problem
   - Includes a project in the student's concentration area

B. Behavioral Science (6 courses)

1. General Psychology
   - Includes perceptual psychology
   - Includes ecological psychology and other phenomenological views of human behavior

2. Cognitive Psychology
   - Includes constraints on human information processing
   - Includes differences between human and machine processing

3. Introduction to Ethnography (an Anthropology course)
   - Includes techniques for the discovery of social and political structures
   - Includes application of techniques to modern groups, such as corporate cultures

4. Qualitative Research Methods
   - Includes development of conceptual models

5. Quantitative Research Methods

6. Elective

C. Computer Science (7 courses)

1.&2. Computer Programming I & II

3. Algorithms and Data Structures

4. Programming Languages or an additional computer language such as COBOL or C
   - Includes object-oriented languages and systems

5. Software Engineering
   - Includes tools and techniques for management of software complexity

6. Artificial Intelligence
   - Includes automatic help systems

7. Computational Linguistics
   - Includes natural language interfaces

M. Mathematics (3 courses)

1.&2. Calculus I & II or a two-course sequence in Business Math

3. Discrete Mathematics
   Includes graph theory, set theory, relations

N. Natural Science (2 courses with accompanying laboratories)

1.&2. Physics I & II or Chemistry I & II or Biology I & II
   Includes experimentation and hypothesis testing as basic forms of knowledge acquisition

B.& A. Business & Administration (5 courses)

1.&2. Economics I & II
   Includes cost/benefit analysis
   Includes introduction to marketing

3. Accounting

4. Introduction to Management
   Includes project management

5. Organizational Behavior
   Includes technological innovation and adoption in organizations.
   Includes end-user computing

A. Arts and Humanities (5 courses)

1&2. Freshman English I & II

3. Technical Writing

4. Effective Speaking

5. Elective

APPENDIX C

A Computer Science Undergraduate Specialization in Human-Computer Interaction (User-centered System and Interface Design)

Ronald Baecker
Department of Computer Science
University of Toronto

This appendix describes a new undergraduate Computer Science specialist program begun by the University of Toronto Computer Science Department in September 1991. This program in human-computer interaction and user-centered system and interface design illustrates how such a program can be embedded within a Computer Science department framework. The special conditions at the University of Toronto underlying this particular curriculum design are first discussed. There follows a complete description of the program, including the goals of the curriculum and a list of course offerings and requirements for an undergraduate degree in the form of a prototypical 4 year schedule. To understand the context in which this curriculum has been developed, it is helpful to read the text of the preceding report. Copies are available from the author of this document. The intellectual foundations of this curriculum have been described in Baecker, Ronald, A Vision of Education in User-centered System and Interface Design, *SIGCHI Bulletin*, 20(3), 10-13.

C.1 Background and Constraints

1) The University of Toronto undergraduate degree in Computer Science is a broad program in both theoretical and applied computer science, but, compared to many other programs, it places particular emphasis on the theory of computation and on

numerical analysis. On the other hand, there are precedents for modifying the program in substantial ways, and the department already supports the following Specialist Programs:

- Specialist program in computer science
- Specialist program in computer science for data management
- Specialist program in computer science and economics
- Specialist program in computer science and mathematics
- Specialist program in applied mathematics and computer science
- Specialist program in computer science and statistics
- Specialist program in computer science and physics
- Specialist program in cognitive science and artificial intelligence

2) All courses in computer science are half courses (1 term long). These are denoted by an H.

3) Most courses in psychology and sociology are full course (1 year, or 2 terms long). These are denoted by a Y.

4) Only 2 courses in "media and design" are offered at the University of Toronto.

C.2 Rationale

Proposals for curricula cannot arise in a vacuum. They must reflect our conceptions of the nature of a field or discipline. They must be grounded in our beliefs about the kinds of graduates we are hoping to produce.

The author of this proposal became involved 2 and 1/2 years ago in the work of an ACM SIGCHI Committee on Curriculum Development for the discipline of human-computer interaction. He began his work by thinking about the nature of the field. The result was the a recognition of the incredible breadth of focus that it implies. How can we do justice to it within a single course or single curriculum? How can we fit the diversity within the confines of an existing discipline such as computer science or psychology? The answers to these questions appear on the following pages.

The field of human-computer interaction is not only a collection of topics spanning interaction techniques to design methodologies, cognitive models to experimental design, organizational issues to physical environments. It is fundamentally a tension between analysis and synthesis, between observation and design, between the emerging science of human-computer interaction and the poorly-understood craft of user-centered system design.

We must seek, therefore, to educate a new generation of system designers, builders, and implementers who are truly sensitive to those who will ultimately use their software. We need students who are sensitive observers and incisive analysts; good conceptual thinkers and sophisticated theory builders; creative, imaginative, and elegant designers and skilled, adept implementers. They should be familiar with a wide variety of relevant disciplines, for example, software engineering and user interface management systems, the psychology of perception and cognitive science, graphic design and industrial design, organization theory and experimental design. They must be able to communicate with users, managers, programmers, psychologists, and graphic designers. They must have a deep commitment to and empathy with the problems of the computer user.

To do this, we need a new kind of curriculum. Instead of just getting experience on toy problems with clear specifications, students need experience designing, building, and evaluating systems that have the fuzzy kinds of specifications that real systems have. In addition to thinking about proving programs correct, students need to understand how to make systems usable, to understand the pervasive problems real users have with most computer systems, and to understand the complexities of the organizational environments in which systems exist and often fail. Instead of learning about theoretical statistics, students need to learn about applied statistics, about the philosophical underpinnings for designing experiments and extracting human behaviour data, and about the kinds of observational techniques that will help them evaluate and improve the systems they design and build. In addition to the techniques of analysis that are stressed by our current program, students need more experience in the disciplines of synthesis, design, and creation of artifacts of many kinds. Finally, in addition to the skills of communication in mathematics and algorithms, our students need practice and improvement in the art of communication in written and spoken English. As professors, we feel an obligation to do something about this. As people who have worked in industry, we see the need.

An HCI specialization within computer science must contain "most" of the contents of a good computer science degree. It must not be viewed as watered-down computer science. It must be an academic degree with a great deal of depth and rigour. We want our graduates to be able to go on to graduate work in human-computer interaction or in other areas of computer science. They should also be well prepared for careers in software development, interface design, or human factors either in software development companies or in corporate environments concerned with the planning, management, implementation, or use of software solutions.

We therefore organize the proposed curriculum in terms of four groups of courses:

- General education (university- or faculty-wide distribution) requirements

Physical science	2 terms
Mathematics	2 terms
Behavioural science	2 terms

- Computer science core requirements

Mathematics	1 term
Computer science	9 terms

- Requirements for the HCI specialization

Human-computer interaction	2 terms
Additional computer science	2 terms
Statistics / research design	4 terms
Psychology and cognitive science	2-4 terms
Social science	2-4 terms
Media and design	8 terms

- Electives — 6 terms
  (Including a course stressing writing in English)

Course Schedule

Year One

...	A first year calculus course (MAT135Y/ 139Y/149Y/150Y)
...	A first year physical science (PHY130Y/ 138Y/150Y)
CSC 148F/158S	Introduction to computing / Computer applications
or	
CSC 150F/160S	Introductory computer science / Applications of computer science
SOC 101Y	Introduction to sociology
or	
yyyH/zzzH	Elective stressing writing in English (ENG103Y, Effective Writing, recommended)

Year Two

MAT 229H	Linear algebra
CSC 238H	Discrete mathematics for computer science
CSC 228H	File structures and data management
CSC 258H	Computer organization
PSY 100Y	Introductory psychology
SOC 200Y	Introduction to social research
xxxY or yyyH/zzzH	Elective

Year Three

CSC 300F	Computers and society
CSC 318S	Introduction to user interface design and

	interactive graphics
CSC 324F	Principles of programming languages
CSC 340S	Information systems analysis and design
CSC 364H	Effective and efficient computing
or CSC 378H	Information structures
PSY 201H/202H	Research design and analysis in psychology I and II
or STA 222Y	Statistics: A general survey
or SOC 300Y	Quantitative analysis
PSY 270H	Introduction to cognitive psychology
or JUP 250Y	Introduction to cognitive science
qqqH	Elective

Year Four

CSC 428F	Human-computer interaction
CSC 364H	Effective and efficient computing
or CSC 378H	Information structures

Two of the following:

CSC 408H	Software engineering
or CSC 418H	Computer graphics
or CSC 448H	Formal languages and automata
or CSC 454S	The business of software
or CSC 468F	Operating systems
or CSC 484S	Applied artificial intelligence
or CSC 485F	Introduction to computational linguistics
or CSC 494H	Computer science project
WDW 260Y	Organizational behaviour
SMC 415Y	Seminar in film and videotape production
or ARC 381Y	Visual studies: towards an understand-

	ing of form
xxxY or yyyH/zzzH	Elective

Some Recommended Electives

Any of the above courses not already taken

ANT 100Y	Introduction to anthropology
IND 205F	Human factors in workplace design
IND 323S	Analysis of man-machine systems
IND 325S	Information display systems
IND 424F	Design of human-machine systems
IND 427S	Human factors: Case studies
NEW 205H	Information skills
PSY 220H	Introduction to social psychology
PSY 280Y	Perception
PSY 370H	Thinking and reasoning
PSY 389Y	Laboratory in perception
SOC 207Y	Sociology of work and occupations
SOC 317Y	Industrial sociology
SOC 375Y	Sociology of organizations
SOC 387Y	Qualitative analysis

C.3 Procedural Matters

The University of Toronto Department of Computer Science Undergraduate Curriculum Committee approved this program in principle in April of 1990 and in its final form in October of 1990. The Faculty of Arts and Science approved it in November of 1990. This program incorporates suggestions made by other members of the university community, especially in psychology, sociology, industrial engineering and media, and by students and individuals from industry. Everyone who has commented has been enthusiastic. The program began in September of 1991.

Students who started in the fall of 1990 can join the program after year one by taking both PSY 100Y and SOC 101Y in year two. Students who started in September of 1989 can join the program after year two by taking SOC 101Y in the summer of 1991, by taking PSY 100Y in 1991-92, by taking SOC 200Y in 1991-92, and by taking CSC 364H or CSC 378H and PSY 270H or JUP 250Y in 1992-93, potentially allowing the first students to graduate in 1993.

APPENDIX D

An Interdisciplinary Undergraduate Specialization in Human-Computer Interaction

Tom Carey
Dept. of Computing and Information Science
University of Guelph

D.1 Developing an interdisciplinary curriculum in Human-Computer Interaction

All computer science students should be exposed to the issues and concerns of human-computer interaction as part of their fundamental courses. Those who have further interest in user interfaces will be served by course material focused specifically on methods and tools in human-computer interaction. There is a further specialization which requires a different approach. Some students will want to combine their computer science knowledge with equivalent expertise in "human sciences", to focus on bridging between users and technology. This requires that we build more effective curriculum bridges between the disciplines which contribute to our understanding of human-computer interaction.

Students who seek to combine the study of two disciplines can often opt for a joint major, offering a selection of courses in the two areas. This could be accomplished for human-computer interaction by majoring in computer science and cognitive science, for example.

There are two limitations with this approach. First, in practice, it is difficult to go beyond the two major disciplines to include other areas of importance to human- computer interaction, because of the breadth requirements within each of the twin majors. Second, the resulting program may be multidisciplinary, but it is not intentionally interdisciplinary. It is up to the student to bring together the material from the two disciplinary perspectives.

An interdisciplinary program in human-computer interaction therefore offers some unique opportunities. First, it reinforces the very nature of human-computer interaction as a multi- dimensional phenomenon. Secondly, an interdisciplinary program could produce graduates who are equally comfortable dealing with technological issues, the needs of individuals and the concerns of their organizations and workgroups. In addition, an interdisciplinary program could prepare students for leadership roles within the development process for interactive systems, integrating the skills and perspectives of a diverse development team.

Three key discipline areas would have to be included: 1) the technological perspective from computer science, 2) the ergonomics issues at an individual level, from cognitive science or human factors curricula, and 3) the "systemic" issues, from disciplines like organizational science, information systems, or sociology. It is the integration of these perspectives which a truly interdisciplinary program would provide.

An interdisciplinary program must be more than a smorgasbord of courses. The courses must be chosen so that students achieve a sense of mastery for each discipline's paradigms. Ideally, they would be able to "think like" software engineers, psychologists, etc., so that their communication with specialists from those disciplines does not flounder on conceptual or terminological differences.

This level of understanding is also necessary within the academic setting: we want the students in human-computer interaction to be respected by faculty from other areas of each disciplines (partly to insure that the study of human-computer interaction is also respected). For all these reasons, the program will have to include breadth within each discipline—although the depth may be restricted to the focus area of HCI.

What about all the other areas which are pertinent to designing effective user interfaces: graphics design, physical ergonomics, technical writing, education and training? Given that no program can cover everything, these will probably have to be treated in a cursory way through isolated electives. The program will focus on the aspects which have the largest design implications, in particular for determining the appropriate roles for users and systems and the information flows between them.

D.2 Assembling a program

In practical terms, a new interdisciplinary program must be built largely out of existing courses in order to be viable. On the other hand, some integrating course seems necessary to bring together the perspectives and issues of the different disciplines. We have drawn up the following sample curriculum as an example of how existing courses can form the basis for an interdisciplinary perspective on human-computer interaction. It is based on a four year course of two semesters a year, with 5 courses per semester. The only new course is the "capstone" integration in the final semester—all the others were taken from a typical university calendar.

A typical mix of courses would be:

Computing and Information Science	11
Psychology	9
Sociology and Anthropology	8
Electives	12
	40

A concrete instantiation of this program is described at the end of this appendix, as a calendar listing from the University of Guelph in Canada. The program in Information Systems and Human Behaviour began there in the fall of 1989.

D.3 Directions

Many current students of human-computer interaction have expressed interest in such a program. There is also substantial interest from potential employers. It appears likely that some form of work-study option would be beneficial for all concerned. This might best take the form of a student internship between the third and fourth years of program. A number of industrial labs offer internships in this form, and a number of academic programs require it (especially in the U.K., where it is known as the "sandwich year").

Perhaps the largest obstacle to successfully mounting such a program is the existing image of computing in the entering student population. The students who have expressed interest in such a program did not enter university with that intent. Their experience of computing in high school sometimes divided the world into two opposing camps: technical wizards with little interest in interpersonal dynamics (a.k.a. nerds), and the rest of us who had to cope with the technology as best we could. The idea that computing careers were available to the "people- oriented" only became evident within their university programs, and often fairly late in the program at that. Integrating HCI concerns and techniques within the computer science curriculum can inform students who have entered a CS program. But we have a lot of work to do to inform students at the high school level, and encourage them with the prospect of nurturing their people skills while contributing to technological development.

D.4 Calendar Description: Information Systems and Human Behavior

As computers and communications play progressively more subtle and significant roles in society, this program of study brings together the elements of three disciplines to provide students an understanding of technical, behavioral and social aspects of the information technology. This program of study is a cooperative effort of the Department of Computing and Information Science, Department of Psychology and Department of Sociology and Anthropology. Students in this program will be counselled by the Academic Counsellor in the Department of Computing and Information Science.

Semester 1

27-150 Introduction to Programming
80-110 Principles of Behavior
86-110 Sociology
Two courses, one each from two different departments in the College of Arts

Semester 2

27-170 Introduction to Computing and Information Science
27-190 Discrete Structures in Computer Science
80-120 Dynamics of Behavior
86-115 Social Anthropology
One course from the College of Arts

Semester 3

27-240 Introduction to Information Systems
80-265 Introduction to Cognitive Processes
80-201 Qualification in Psychology or 89-204 Statistics I
86-212 Introductory Methods in Sociology
One elective

Semester 4

27-242 Data Structures
80-239 Principles of Perception
80-236 Introductory Experimental Methods in Psychology
86-307 Qualitative and Observational Methods
One elective (26-140 Introduction to Design recommended)

Semester 5

27-360 Programming Languages
27-343 Information System Analysis and Design
86-204 Sociology of Work or 80-231 Introduction to Social Psychology
Two electives (85-250 Management in Organizations recommended)

Semester 6

80-334 Psycholinguistics or 80-333 Human Memory

80-351 Industrial-Organizational Psychology
or 86-306 Organizations
86-320 Technology and Society
27-320 Software Engineering I: Software Design and Development
One elective

Semester 7

27-430 Human-Computer Interaction
One 400 level course in Sociology or Psychology
One 400 level Computing and Information Science course
Two electives (38-310 Teaching and Learning in Non-Formal Education recommended)

Semester 8

27-444 Software Engineering II: Software Project Management
86-429 Applied Sociology and Anthropology
or 400 level course in Sociology
80-440 Contemporary Issues in Sensory, Perceptual and Cognitive Processes or 400 level course in Psychology
Two electives (74-360 Business and Professional Ethics recommended)

DEPARTMENT OF COMPUTER SCIENCE
UNIVERSITY OF TORONTO

CSC 428F / 2514 F
Human-Computer Interaction

Fall Term 1989

Assignment 3

Topic: The detailed human behaviour evaluation of a user interface analogous to the new interface design being developed.

Handed Out: Friday, October 13, 1988
Due: Friday, November 3, 1988

Objectives of Assignment:

The objective of this assignment is to give Computer Science students practice in evaluating human-computer interfaces since a large part of their future work will be directed at building such interfaces. This practice is intended to help them in developing evaluation criteria appropriate to the interface. The evaluation, in turn can guide their design decisions.

Because the purpose of the exercise is to develop skills which later can be applied to interface design, the student is expected to focus on the very detailed issues that arise in design; for example, whether a transpose two characters command should be available in a text editor or whether a "t" for "transpose" or "x" for "exchange" should be used as the command to transpose the characters. This means developing evaluation criteria and miniature experiments/tests to evaluate the user interface at this level.

The assignment also has three sub-objectives. The first of these is to give students practice in the detailed observation of users at work with interfaces. Analysis of the user behaviour is intended to give the students skills in observing humans at the micro-level needed for understanding user problems.

The second sub-objective is to alert computer scientists to very basic differences in user behaviour and to the multiple ways users will interpret information presented to them and generate what is to them, very intelligent guesses about what is needed to use the interface.

One of the basic assumptions that humans have about their counterparts is that we all think alike. This is far from the truth, especially with the differences in skilled training that occur in today's society. When a computer scientist sees the word "print," the word usually means to send an electronic document to a printer. The rest of the world thinks that "print" means to carefully write letters by hand or to produce books. With these definitions, it is very likely for a new user to think that the person who wrote the instructions "now, *print your file*," in a user manual is asking for extremely bizarre behaviour.

The third sub-objective is to give students practice in distinguishing between the functionality of a computer system and its usability. The computer system may do all the tasks that the user needs to perform with the system, but may be required to organize the steps to perform these tasks in an order which is extremely foreign to the way the user thinks about the tasks.

For example, in text editing, the user typically has to mark the beginning and end of the text to be deleted. When an edit is done manually with a pencil, a word is indicated for delete by drawing a line partially through the word and ending it with a "squiggle" that indicates remove. The computer text editor may require the user to position a cursor at both ends of the word. This double positioning has added an additional mental task to the mental delete procedure of the user.

Without Computer:	<find word> <indicate delete>
With Computer:	<find word start> <find word end> <indicate delete>

The delete function is available to the user, but its usability is questionable. With enough such extra thinking processes added to each function, the user might be better off using a typewriter which is within the cognitive capabilities of humans.

NOTE: This assignment is focussed only on the usability analysis of the interface not on the what functions might be needed for the new design. It is assumed that this functionality was captured in Assignment 1.

Directions:

This assignment will have **5** steps. They are:

1. Develop at least **3** criteria for evaluating your analogous interface.
2. Conduct the evaluation of the interface.
3. Analyze the results of the evaluation.
4. Write up the evaluation indicating what was good and what was bad about the evaluated interface.
5. Suggest ways in which the results of the evaluation can be applied to your interface design.

<u>You should turn in:</u>

A **four** page (maximum) write-up on the evaluations that were conducted. The write-up should include, **in order**, the following items.

1. A brief description of your analogous interface and the interface you are designing. You can copy this from your previous assignments.

2. A discussion of the evaluation criteria. The criteria should be related to how the interface is used or perceived, e.g., one obvious use of the Felix System is to search for books.

3. A discussion of the tests you took to perform the comparisons, e.g., you could calculate how long it took each of the subjects to perform a typical task in the interface.

4. A report on the evaluation conducted. What was good about the design of the interface and what functions appear to cause great difficulties. Your interface evaluation should be tied to the information you gathered not just to your intuitive impression of the interface. You need justification for your critique.

5. Recommendations for your own design based on the evaluation. It may be that your analogous interface performed superbly. In this case, you should say so and indicate what good features you should bring over to your design.

Oral Presentation Requirements:

You should be prepared to give a presentation of your evaluation and its results in your tutorial sessions on either October 27th or November 3rd. Be prepared to answer questions about your evaluation tests and your recommendations

Your presentations must be clear and well organized. Use overheads to show your main points and your conclusions. Fifty percent of your class participation grade will be based on your presentations.

Expect your presentations to be 8 minutes long. You will be given an additional 2 minutes at the end to answer questions.

Written Presentation Requirements:

Your paper must be typed on 8.5 x 11 inch paper. Figures and graphs must be clear and legible. Be sure to put on a cover page indicating your name, title of work, course and date. You will be judged on the visual appearance, grammatical correctness and quality of writing of your paper as well as its contents.

Only the first **four** pages of the paper will be read and graded. This does not include references, figures or tables. Papers should have 1 inch left, right, top and bottom margins. They must be text with paragraphs, full sentences and all the other appurtenances of a written presentation. They cannot be itemized lists of points. Text font size should be either 10 or 12 points. You may choose your own font style, but a serif font is preferred.

Hints for Selecting Evaluation Criteria:

Below are a series of suggested evaluation mechanisms that you might consider in performing Assignment 3. The list is far from complete and although you are welcome to use these hints, it is important to develop your own criteria as well.

LEARNING:

1. How easy is analogous interface to learn?
2. Do the commands have a structure or organization that makes learning easier?
3. Do the commands relate to English words which describe the same task?
4. Are the commands discriminable, e.g., are they whole words or single letter commands?

TASK USABILITY:

1. Are various functions of the interface easily done by the users or does a simple task take long and involved steps?
2. Are there functions that users would never use because they are infrequent and need to be looked up each time?
3. Can the user build in shortcuts once the interface is learned?
4. Are there functions that do not match any task a user might wish to do?

DOCUMENTATION:

1. How easy is it to read the documentation? Is the manual so long and cumbersome that a user will never take the time to read it?
2. Is it easy to find the commands to perform a particular task or do you have to reference many different places in the manual?
3. Does the manual use words which have a different meaning for the user?
4. Does the interface provide reminders of what to do next so that the manual does not have to be constantly referred to?
5. Is the on screen help slow and cumbersome? Does it help?

OVERALL USABILITY:

1. Is the interface cluttered with too much detail so that it is difficult for the user to see what is going on?

2. Does the interface provide feedback to the user indicating that a command has been received and is now being executed?

3. Can the user get into situations in using the interface that allow no easy exit?

Hints for Implementing Evaluation Criteria:

In addition to setting up the evaluation criteria, you must use it. Here are some hints for implementing LEARNING item 1 into evaluation tests.

1. Set up a test to see how long it takes to learn part of the user interface:

   Build a set of tasks, e. g., in searching for books in the FELIX System, it might be handwritten notes on titles, authors and subjects to look at in researching a course paper. You would then learn a subset of FELIX's commands. Do this by mentally rehearsing the command set. Time yourself. When you think you have mastered the command set, look at your set of your handwritten notes and write down beside each one, the set of commands you would do to perform the search. Try to do the same thing the next day.

   Have one of your colleagues in class learn an equivalent set of commands for the other editor. The colleague should perform the same tests on the same set of editing corrections. Compare the times and errors.

2. Measure how many things there are to learn:

   List a set of basic tasks that your analogous interface must do for anyone beginning to use it. Count the number of commands you will need to learn to perform these tasks.

   For a more detailed measurement, add 10 to your count every time a different format for the command needs to be learned.

3. Measure how easy the commands are for novices to learn:

   Teach a friend who knows nothing about computing two of the interface commands. Ask them to explain how the commands work after you feel that you have adequately described the command. Ask them to describe as many situations as they can in which they believe the commands can be used. Write down any conceptual errors they make in expressing their understanding of the commands.

DEPARTMENT OF COMPUTER SCIENCE
UNIVERSITY OF TORONTO

CSC 428F / 2514 F
Human-Computer Interaction

Fall Term, 1988-89

Assignment 4

Topic: The design of a prototype of your chosen user interface using Apple Macintosh HyperCard as your rapid prototyping system

Handed Out: Friday, November 3, 1988
Due: Friday, November 17, 1988

Objectives of Assignment:

The objective of this assignment is to combine the various skills and techniques that have been learned in this course to a user interface design problem. In Assignment 1 a methodology for finding out information about the user population was practiced. With Assignment 2, practice was gained in modeling the user's interaction with a proposed design. Assignment 3 provided practice in observing users and relating the user's behaviour to the design of your proposed interface. Assignment 4 asks you to apply all of these skills to making a HyperCard prototype of your proposed interface.

The assignment also has a sub-objective, that of giving practice in developing a "good" user interface within the constraints of the design environment. The classic constraint in user interface design is the small amount of time allowed to build an acceptable interface for the user. Due dates for this assignment impose a similar constraint requiring decisions about which user interface features that can be included in the design given the minimal amount of time available. A second constraint—as common as the first—is the constraints of the external user, the software and the hardware environments. User interface designs need to adapt to the history of prior interfaces, to the consistency requirements of similar interfaces and to the limitations of the hardware and development software that will be used. To simulate a portion of these constraints, you are being asked to design a prototype of your system in HyperCard.

Directions:

Your basic task is to design a prototype of your proposed user interface in Apple Macintosh's HyperCard system. The design will not be an implementation. You will use HyperCard to create mock-ups of your design. If, for example, your design contains a videodisk, a HyperCard window with some sort of animation in it that simulates the video playback from the videodisk would be appropriate.

You are expected to apply the information you have gathered about your intended user in the three previous assignments, to your design.

This assignment will have 8 steps. They are:

1. Develop a set of design criteria about what the interface should provide for its users. This is more than the typical requirements list for software design. In addition to describing the functions the system should perform, the design criteria should contain user information.

   For example, if you were designing a calendar system, your design criteria might be, "have appointment book open to current date because this is the date that is most frequently accessed by the user." Use the information from Assignments 1, 2 and 3 to aid in developing this design criteria.

2. Sketch out your design on paper. You may sketch out more than one design. For each design, be sure that it is described in enough detail so that users can see screen display changes and individual inputs that they would need to make if they were using the designed interface.

3. Elicit user input and changes on your design. You can query your friends, parents, colleagues or significant others.

4. Repeat steps 2 and 3, adapting your design to match what you have learned about the design from showing it to potential users.

5. Draw out your design both in terms of screen displays and state transition diagrams showing user actions. (Use the paper on pages 508-527 to learn how to draw a user interface state transition diagram.)

6. Learn Hypertalk well enough to develop screen layouts for your design. You are not being asked to build a complete implementation of your design, but enough of a prototype to demonstrate the design to users.

7. Build a mock-up of your design in HyperCard. Build a storyboard (different screen displays with descriptions of user actions below the displays). Have these storyboards describe a sequence of user interactions with the system. Expect to use the storyboards in Assignment 5 to run your usability studies.

8. Write up your design including a description of the processes you went through in making the design follow the needs and psychology of the user.

<u>You should turn in:</u>

A diskette containing your mock-up of the appointment page design. It should be a HyperCard stack. Call the stack **CSC428 Design**.

A maximum of **five** pages write-up on the design process that was conducted. The write-up should include, in order, the following items.

1. A description of the final design. This should be presented in enough detail so that it is possible for a programmer to implement the design. Use printouts of specific screens to show what the user will see and the actions available to the user at each state. List the design criteria that produced this design in the process in your description.

2. A state transition diagram showing the user actions at each state of the system and the transitions that take place following the user actions. Use the model described by Wasserman et al. on pages 508-527 of Baecker and Buxton for drawing your state transition diagram.

3. A discussion of the user information you used to create your design, e.g., data from the papers you read on people's use of similar systems, your own studies of people's use of analogous systems, your keystroke level model calculations comparing alternative designs or information gleaned from the questionnaires you administered. This discussion should contain the psychological as well as functional aspects of the task.

   For example, if you were designing a calendar system, you might include the functional information that people write down multiple appointments occurring at the same time (if this is true) and use this information to keep track of what other people are doing, not just what their appointments are. As psychological data you might indicate that people have trouble with the limited amount of space available and often put down abbreviated information which is indecipherable at a later date (if you find this to be true.)

4. A conclusion describing what is good about your design and what you are not very happy with but have had to include in the design given the constraints of the design problem and the trade-off decisions you needed to make.

   HINT: All previous assignments have prepared you for this design assignment. Look back at the evaluations you have performed and transfer the concepts in these evaluations to evaluating your design.

   You will be graded on the **quality** of your user interface, the **creativeness** of your design in solving the user interface problems you encountered and your ability to **incorporate** into the design process, the user data you collected in Assignments 1, 2 and 3.

Oral Presentation Requirements:

You should be prepared to give a presentation of your design in the tutorial sessions. The presentation should include pictures of what you plan your design to look like and descriptions of actions you expect the users of your interface to take. Bring your diskette for your presentation. We will have a video connection to a Macintosh computer set up for you to demo your system design.

Your presentations must be clear and well organized. Use HyperCard screens to show your main points and your conclusions. Five percent of your grade will be based on your presentation. Expect your presentations to be exactly 8 minutes long. You will be given an additional 2 minutes at the end to answer questions and receive feedback from classmates on your design. You will need to be able to justify the functionality and usability of your design. Class members are expected to critique the design in the question portion of the presentation.

Written Presentation Requirements:

The written presentation requirements are the same as those for previous Assignments.

DEPARTMENT OF COMPUTER SCIENCE
UNIVERSITY OF TORONTO

CSC 428F / 2514 F
Human-Computer Interaction

Fall Term, 1988-89

Assignment 5

Topic: The evaluation of the prototype of your user interface design by means of a usability study

Handed Out: Friday, November 10, 1989
Due: Friday, December 1, 1989

Objectives of Assignment:

The objective of this assignment is to give students practice in the detailed observation of problems users have with human-computer interfaces. The practice is intended to give them experience in knowing what elements of behaviour to look for and how to categorize this behaviour so that they can draw conclusions from it about problems with a particular user interface design.

Directions:

Your basic task is to evaluate the HyperCard prototype of your proposed user interface.

This assignment will have 10 steps. They are:

1. Sign up for a time slot to use the HCI Laboratory (Room 4302SF). Learn how to use video gear in your November 24th tutorial session.

2. Develop a set of user instructions and tasks for a user to perform as part of your videotaping session (usability study).

3. Prepare a short questionnaire that obtains useful demographic information on your subject, e.g., level of education, sex, amount of computer experience. Add a set of questions to determine user satisfaction with your interface.

4. Run your trial sessions of your instructions and tasks with representative users of your system in order to determine if the tasks will fit within your half-hour videotaping time slot. Based on the trial session, adjust the instructions and tasks accordingly.

Note: Although you will have one-half an hour to perform your videotaping, you will probably have a maximum of 15 minutes of videotape that you can capture because of the time that will be spent in setting up the study.

5. Obtain a subject for your usability study and bring this person along to the videotaping session. You may also use one of the *Designated Subjects* in this class.

   Note: It is best to have a subject that has very little computer experience since the interfaces you are building are for such individuals. You will also learn much more about your interface design if you use a subject who has had little, if any, previous computer experience. A computer science student may give you very little to write your evaluation about.

6. Videotape your subject attempting to use your user interface. You may videotape a second subject at a different time if there are open sign up slots for doing so.

   Note: If you are presenting a videotape of your subject in class you will need to obtain signed permission to do so from your subject.

7. Administer your demographic and user satisfaction questionnaire to your subject.

8. Replay your videotape and analyze the subject's interaction with your interface. To perform this analysis, you will need to look for **critical incidents** and **user misconceptions** about the interface. Also look for such things as the number of errors your subject made and the amount of time it took them to complete tasks compared to the amount of time you estimated for each task. Expect to scan the videotape slowly and more quickly to get very micro and very macro levels of behaviour.

9. Develop a set of improvements to your design based on its user evaluation. You do not need to implement these improvements in your HyperCard prototype, only to make the recommendations.

10. Write up your usability study including a description of the changes you need to make to your design if it is to follow the needs and psychology of the user.

<u>You should turn in:</u>

A videotape cassette containing a usability study of your prototype design. The videotape should be 1/2 inch VHS.

A maximum of **four** pages write-up on the design process that was conducted. The write-up should include, in order, the following items.

1. A short description of the user interface design you are testing.

2. A description of the user problems you observed in your usability studies. You will need to describe these problems in detail.

3. A categorization of the observed user problems and a set of recommendations for changing your design.

4. A conclusion summarizing what is good about your design and what difficulties you expect users will have with the final system based on your observations. At this point, you may even suggest that the entire design be scrapped and redone. This will depend on your usability study results.

   You will be graded on the **quality** of your evaluation and your **insight** into human behaviour you are observing.

Oral Presentation Requirements:

You should be prepared to give a presentation of your evaluation in the tutorial sessions. The presentation should include appropriate segments from your videotape to demonstrate your evaluation conclusions.

Your oral presentation requirements are the same as those for previous Assignments.

Written Presentation Requirements:

The written presentation requirements are the same as those for previous Assignments.

Materials Available for this Assignment:

Videotaping facilities will be available in the HCI Laboratory adjacent to the Dynamic Graphics Project (Room 4302 SF) in addition to a Mac II on which to run your HyperCard prototype. These videotape facilities will be available on Friday, November 24th through Monday, November 27th. You will need to check in with the secretary in Room 4303 SF five minutes before your scheduled time to run your experiment. In return for your student card, she will give you access to the laboratory and the videotaping equipment. Plan on having a half hour to set up your experiment and execute it with your subject. You will not be given write access to the hard disk of the Mac II.

If you do not have access to a VCR, you may analyze your videotape by using the VCRs in Sigmund Samuel Library.

DEPARTMENT OF COMPUTER SCIENCE
UNIVERSITY OF TORONTO

CSC 428F / 2514 F
Human-Computer Interaction

October 20, 1989

Midterm Examination

Name:______________________________ Student No.: ______________________________

Directions:

Put your name and student number in the space provided above. You will have **50 minutes** to complete the examination. **No** questions will be answered during the exam. If you find a question ambiguous, document the ambiguity and indicate which way you interpreted the question in a separate set of sentences next to the question. The questions on the exam are not intended to be ambiguous, but sometimes another meaning is interpreted by the examinee that the creator of the exam did not take into consideration.

Two caveats exist for documenting ambiguities:

1. Do not take too much of your examination time to do so and

2. Do not trivialize the question, i.e., interpret it in a fashion so that the answer is extremely easy.

Part I - Short Essay Answers (2 questions at 10 points each) _____

Part II - Long Essay Answers (2 questions at 15 points each) _____

Total Score _____

Part I - Short Essay Answers - 2 Questions at 10 points each

Answer the questions in 2-4 paragraphs. If you write LARGE, use the space on the opposing page, but be sure to indicate clearly what question number your answer refers to.

1. As part of your assigned material, you read a case study on the introduction of information technology in a biscuit making factory. In the case study, two jobs were affected by the technology introduction, that of the doughman and that of the ovenman.

   a. **Describe** the impact of the change on these two groups of employees.
   b. **Indicate** the employees satisfaction or dissatisfaction with the change in these two groups.
   c. **Explain** why the workers' levels of satisfaction were different for the two positions.
   d. **Describe** how the computer system might have been designed differently to make both sets of workers content.

2. A system designer has in mind an office workflow system where each individual will list the work he or she needs to do that day, week or month. Each individual will also list the work required from other people. The system will then determine the daily work that each person in the office is to do and suggest a set of daily tasks to each individual when they login in the morning. The tasks will be organized to optimize the flow of work through the office.

   For example, John may list as one of his tasks, "incorporate waste management calculations in final budget." He may also list that he needs the figures for last year's waste management costs from Judy. The computer will then put on Judy's schedule the task of providing John with last year's waste management figures. If John needs to finish the budget by Friday, this may be the first thing that Judy will be required to do on Monday morning.

   The system designer wants to know how workers in an office will react to this type of control of their workflow. He has written the following two questions to provide him with this information.

   a. I agree with my supervisor and think it is a good idea for a computer to control the order in which I perform my work.

1	2	3	4	5
Strongly Agree	Agree	Neutral	Disagree	Strongly Disagree

   b. Please list any tasks in the last year that you have had to wait for work to be finished by one of your co-workers. For each task indicate how many days you had to wait.

(space is provided here in the questionnaire for listing tasks)

Critique the two questions in terms of what you know about how to design questions that will give valid answers from users. **List** two precautions you need to take in the generation of questions which determine people's attitudes towards things, i.e., what kinds of common question design mistakes do you need to look out for.

Part II - Long Essay Answers - 2 Questions at 15 points each

Answer the questions in 4-5 paragraphs. If you write LARGE, use the space on the opposing page, but be sure to indicate clearly what question number your answer refers to.

3. Suppose that you are asked to design a change to a mouse-based visual screen text editor (Macintosh - like) to make the task of finding and making global changes to a document easier. Suppose that the current method for finding and changing a string anywhere in the document is done by:

Design 1

1. Put the hand on the mouse.
2. Select the *Change* option by pointing to *Search* in a pull-down menu, hold down the mouse key and drag the pointer to the value *Change* and lift up on the mouse key.
3. Put the hand back on the keyboard.
4. Type the string to be changed in the box provided on the screen (the cursor is already positioned correctly) and hit <carriage return>.
5. Type the new string (again the cursor is in the correct position) and hit <carriage return>.

   The text editor, at this point, finds every match to the change string and displays the section of the text with the string to be changed highlighted in reverse video. For each of the found strings, the user is required to okay or not okay the change. If the change is okayed, it will be made. If not, it will be ignored only for that particular match. The process of okaying each change continues until all found string matches have been displayed or until the user types <q> for quit.

6. Type a <y> to verify that the change is okay for each string in the document. If the change is not okay, type an <n> for no. If no more changes are to be displayed, type a <q>.

For each string in the document in which a change is confirmed, the string will be changed to the new string.

Suppose that the new method being suggested is done by:

Design 2

1. Type the sequence *<ctrl> C* - hold down the control key while striking the C key. Whenever a <ctrl> <character> sequence is typed, the cursor is moved to a one-line window at the bottom of the document to receive additional command information.

2. Type the string to be changed and hit <carriage return>. (Note that the cursor is positioned in a one-line window at the bottom of the document to receive this information.)

3. Type the new string and hit <carriage return> (Note that the cursor is positioned in a one line window at the bottom of the document to receive this information.)

   The text editor at this point finds each match and performs the change without displaying information to the user. If the user wishes to see the changes made, he or she can type <ctrl> R to review the changes.

4. Type the sequence *<ctrl> R* in order to review changes.

   The text editor, displays each line changed (one at a time) in the window at the bottom of the screen. The change that was made is highlighted in reverse video. Each change made is displayed for 0.5 seconds.

5. If the change is inappropriate, typing a *u* for undo during the line's display will undo the change made. A user can *Review* the last global change made as many times as he or she wishes.

Which of these methods is **shorter** for the user to perform? **Describe** why it is shorter and **show** the calculations that can be made to support your argument.

NOTE: You can use the following average times in your calculations.

Time for a keystroke or button press (avg. typist)	0.28 sec
Time to point to a target with a mouse1	0.10 sec
Time to home hands on keyboard	0.40 sec
Time to mentally prepare for action	1.35 sec
Response time for Design 1	0.30 sec
Response time for Design 2	0.50 sec

4. Below are listed in boldface the basic steps of the User Factors Software Lifecycle. Select any two stages and **describe** the **type** of information about human behaviour that is captured at each of these stages and the **purpose** for collecting and analyzing this information (i.e., how can the information be used to help in the design and development of the software. **Compare** and **contrast** the two stages you have selected to de-

scribe in terms of:

1. The different human behaviour disciplines that would be drawn upon for methods to collect and analyze the information.
2. The methods that would be used for the information collection.
3. The trustworthiness of the data being collected.

Describe in detail at least **one** method that might be used in each one of the two stages you have selected.

Market Analysis
|
Feasibility Study
|
Requirements Definition
|
Product Acceptance Analysis
|
Task Analysis
|
Global Design
|
Prototype Construction
|
User Testing and Evaluation
|
System Implementation
|
Product Testing
|
User Testing
|
Update and Maintenance
|
Product Survey

DEPARTMENT OF COMPUTER SCIENCE
UNIVERSITY OF TORONTO

CSC 428F / 2514 F
Human-Computer Interaction

Fall Term, 1989

Final Exam

Directions:

Put your name and student number in the upper right hand corner of each page. You will have **one hour and 30 minutes** to complete the examination. **No** questions will be answered during the exam. If you find a question ambiguous, document the ambiguity and indicate which way you interpreted the question in a separate set of sentences next to the question. The questions on the exam are not intended to be ambiguous, but sometimes another meaning is interpreted by the examinee that the creator of the exam did not take into consideration.

Two caveats exist for documenting ambiguities:

1. Do not take too much of your examination time to do so and

2. Do not trivialize the question, i.e., interpret it in a fashion so that the answer is extremely easy.

Part I: Multiple Choice (10 questions at 2 points each) _____

Part II: Short Answers (3 questions at 10 points each) _____

Part III: Essay (1 question - 3 parts at 10 points each) _____

Total Score _____

Part I - Multiple Choice: 10 questions at 2 points each

In the following questions, circle the answer which best completes the sentence. Although several statements may seem correct, only one answer will be most correct.

1. Unit tasks

    a. are used to characterize a user's learning process when they using a computer for the first time.
    b. are an important part of analyzing the performance time of human using computer systems for problem solving work
    c. always have an acquisition, a comprehension and an execution portion.
    d. are tasks which only require one operation to perform.
    e. arise because of the cognitive limitations of the human processor.

2. The experiments on the Star user interface demonstrated that

    a. even a psychologist's intuition about a design may be wrong.
    b. design trade-offs will not occur if careful experiments are run.
    c. a large amount of the detailed design decisions which occur in the interface design process are unimportant.
    d. the motor skill for controlling the number of mouse clicks can be taught with 2 days practice.
    e. the most important part of icon design is making each icon visible when it is highlighted.

3. The Keystroke Level Model

    a. only works because keystrokes take longer than any other process, e.g., mental preparation, homing, etc. to perform.
    b. is a subset of the GOMS model.
    c. can be used effectively to build interfaces that are easier to learn.
    d. is used to determine whether QWERTY organized keyboards are better than DVORAK organized keyboards
    e. cannot be applied if a mouse is part of the user interface

4. External Validity

    a. refers to the inherent truthfulness of participants in a questionnaire survey.
    b. refers to user interfaces that have been tested and modified to match the needs of the user. These interfaces are ready to be distributed and are said to have "external validity."
    c. refers to the careful design and administration of an experiment to insure that valid data is obtained.
    d. refers to the generalization of the results obtained in an experiment to the real world population, i.e., is this generalization valid?

e. can never be assured in user interface studies because of the complexity of the experimental design.

5. A dependent variable

   a. is an amount that can be deducted from your income tax.
   b. never changes once the experiment begins.
   c. is always measured as time or number of errors.
   d. refers to a measurement taken during or after the experiment and believed to change as a direct or indirect result of the experiment stimulus.
   e. refers to one of the types of treatments that are administered or controlled for in an experiment, e.g., age, type of interface design, etc.

6. When users read a manual to learn how to use a computer system, they are likely to:

   a. learn the material more thoroughly than users who receive formal instruction.
   b. build unexpected interpretations from the manual descriptions.
   c. become frustrated because the examples do not match the tasks they wish to accomplish with the system.
   d. jump the gun and read other parts of the manual before being told to do so.
   e. blame the manual or the manual writer when things are poorly explained.

7. From the set below, select the best question for obtaining a user's honest assessment of whether the new computer system helped them perform their work more efficiently.

   a. Compared to other computer systems you have used, this system is:

1	2	3	4	5
Far Worse	Worse	About Equal	Better	Much Better

   b. What difficulties, if any, do you have with using this system?

   c. This system was designed to make your work more efficient. Has it done so for you? How?

   d. Think back to a time just before the current system was installed. Where there tasks that you disliked doing that you now enjoy doing? If so, what are they and why do you now enjoy doing them?

   e. Please list the number of hours you used to spend on the following tasks and the number of hours you now spend on these same tasks with the new computer system.

	Old Method	With New Computer System
Correcting Text	________	________
Typing New Text	________	________
Duplicating	________	________
Data Entry	________	________

8. A verbal protocol analysis

   a. is an effective method for determining whether one design is better than another design.
   b. is a verbalization of an individual's thought processes as they execute a routine task.
   c. is an especially effective technique for evaluating an expert's performance.
   d. is a study of the verbalizations of an individual's thought processes given while executing a problem solving task.
   e. can only be used in the evaluation and testing stages of the user interface development process.

9. The ability to generate a prototype of the user interface with a user interface management system

   a. has seriously undermined the programming morale of software projects.
   b. can provide significant cost savings in the design phase of the software project.
   c. is essential for the effective development of usable user interfaces.
   d. has created an entirely new class of interfaces based on graphics and windows
   e. is best described by items b and c above.

10. Metaphors are used in the design of user interfaces

   a. to simulate the phosphorous behaviour of video screens on less luminous LCD panels.
   b. to cause the interface to behave like an office environment, e.g., the desktop metaphor.
   c. to replace simple command languages which are inadequate for providing the full functionality of the interface.
   d. to help the user by placing the context of the interface into a context already known by the user.
   e. to relate the user interface to similar tasks that the user has performed with computer systems.

Part II - Short Answer - 3 Questions at 10 points each

Answer the following questions in 1-3 paragraphs. If you write LARGE, use the space on the opposing page, but be sure to indicate clearly what question number your answer refers to.

11. User Interface Management Systems are based on the belief that you can separate the operation of the user interface from the workings of the underlying program. For example, a UIMS allows a designer to quickly set up the keypad and display area for a prototype calculator. This prototype will accept input selections from the user and send them to an underlying program. The program then performs the numerical calculations being requested and sends the answer back to the user interface part of the program to be displayed. **Explain** why this separation of the underlying application code from the interface is not always possible. Give at least **one** example of a useful user interface design for which a separation of the user interface code and the application code will not work effectively.

12. **Define** "Direct Manipulation." In your definition **give** at least **two** examples of interface operations that are direct manipulation operations and **two** counter examples for the same type of operations that are not direct manipulation.

13. The user interface to most text editing systems allows the user to find, create, delete and replace text usually with a series of specific keystrokes that identify the actions desired and sometimes through the use of a mouse pointing and dragging arrangement. They also permit the user to retrieve, save and print versions of edited text. Given what you know about auditory interfaces and the human use of sound, design **three** ways in which sound might be added to a text editor interface to enhance its usability. **Describe** these three designs and explain why they enhance the interface. Then design **two** mechanisms for adding sound to the interface which would not be useful for the user and **discuss** why these uses of sound would add little or no value to the interface.

Part III - Long Answer - 30 points - Each part is worth 10 points

Write approximately a page of text in reply to the information requested in each question. If you write on an opposing page be sure to indicate clearly which question you are answering by (1) circling the question number and (2) putting the question number in front of your answer.

14. The attached document describes a user interface to a microwave oven. The first page illustrates the oven control panel which is located to the right of the oven door. For brevity, parts of the user manual have been eliminated, but can be inferred from the explanations of multi-stage and delay start cooking.

(a) Critique the user interface to this microwave oven based on the key concepts of design presented by Norman, i.e., the design's affordance, constraints, mappings, conceptual models, visibility and feedback. List both design features which are good and which are bad in your critique and **support** your commentary with psychological theory or experimental results learned in the course.

(b) Redesign the interface so that it eliminates the problems you have mentioned. Be sure to **indicate** in writing how the redesign will remove the problems. If some of the problems are trade-offs between designs which make it easier for the user in one way but interfere with the user in another way, then **discuss** these trade-offs in your answer.

(c) Draw a state transition diagram that represents your new design and sketch enough of the oven control panel that you designed so that it is understandable to the reader of this exam. Note: It is not necessary to write a user manual, just to make the design you had in mind clear.

APPENDIX F

Case Studies in Human-Computer Interaction

Marilyn Mantei
Department of Computer Science
University of Toronto

A. Case Studies Used in the Example

1. The development of an integrated word processor, spreadsheet and database program for the Amiga microcomputer in a small start-up company.

2. The development of a computer assisted instruction package for building animated tutorials for chemical engineering students.

B. Classic Types of Problems in User Interface Design

1. Scope of task is defined as anything associated with human element.
2. Areas of effort between software developers and human factors personnel in conflict.
3. Representations and tools for design decisions.
4. Not enough theory to drive design decisions.
5. Technology oriented culture not supportive of human factors.

C. Areas of Human Factors Effort in Designing Human Factored Software

1. Identifying who the users of the software product will be.
2. Setting software functionality - what the intended goals of the user will be when employing the software aide.
3. Designing the user interface to the product.
4. Testing the user interface.

D. The Traditional Software Lifecycle

1. Feasibility Study
2. Requirements Definition
3. Design
4. Prototype Construction
5. User Evaluation
6. System Implementation
7. Testing
8. Update and Maintenance

E. Applying the Human Factors Tasks to the Traditional Software Lifecycle

	Software Lifecycle	Human Factors Tasks
1.	Feasibility Study	Defining User
2.	Requirements Definition	Setting Functionality
3.	Design	Designing User Interface
4.	Prototype Construction	Designing User Interface
5.	User Evaluation	Testing User Interface
6.	System Implementation	
7.	Testing	Testing User Interface
8.	Update and Maintenance	Defining User

Case Study 1: What are We Doing, Really?

Background Material

Company: Star-tronics
- 20 Employees
- Product: Software

Sources of Income:
- Sales from Sprite
- Venture Capital
- Equity Arrangements
- Porting Agreements
- Marketing: Via Co-op Contracts
- Organizations Chart for Star-tronics

Description of Perky

- Microprocessor Software
- Integrated Spreadsheet, Word processor and DBMS
- Icon and Mouse Based
- Built-in Tutorial
- Creative Use of Color
- "Cute"

Human Factors Role

- Give Advice on the Design of Perky
  - 0 Answer Detailed Design Questions
  - 0 Build Tutorial
  - 0 Decide on Templates
- Advise HF Sprite Changes
  - 0 Manual Development
  - 0 On-line Tutorial Writing
  - 0 User Testing of Changes

Example of Perky Detailed Design Questions

- Under what circumstances should the integrity of a paragraph be maintained when performing text insertion?

- Should we constantly adjust lines during insertion or should we wait until insertion is an entire line?

- Should we distribute spaces in line evenly for right-adjusted text or should we place spaces near long words?

1. What areas of the Human Factors Software Lifecycle need to be addressed?

___ Defining User
___ Setting Functionality
___ Designing User Interface
___ Testing User Interface

2. Who is the Star-tronics Customer?

Obtaining Information on the User
- 0 Existing Data Bases
- 0 Questionnaires
- 0 Interviews
- 0 Focus Groups
- 0 Observation
- 0 Case Study

User Information Gathered

- Attitudes toward Computers
- Social and Economic Status
- Attitudes toward Tasks to be Supported by Software
- Time Use Patterns
- Usage of Existing Systems

Interaction with Software Development Team

- Redo Management Structure to co-lead Perky Project
- Teach Weekly Human Factors Seminar
- Base Human Factors Seminar on Existing Product Built by Team
- Ask for Amount of Effort Estimate on Each Design Change Requested
- Serve as Management Go-between
- Stay away from Programming

Answering Detailed Design Questions

- Does Decision Affect Product Image?
- Does Decision Affect Interface Consistency?
- Does Decision Affect Completion Time?
- Does Decision Affect Other Parts of Programs?

If none of the above, let software team make decision!

IF USER BASE IS DISCRETIONARY, LET PRODUCT IMAGE GOVERN THE DESIGN DECISION

IF TRAINING TIMES A SIGNIFICANT ISSUE, LET INTERFACE CONSISTENCY GOVERN DESIGN DECISION

Choosing Templates for Perky

- Brainstorming Groups
    - 0 Videotape/CD lists
    - 0 Hobby lists
    - 0 Direct line to bank
    - 0 Personal letter writing
    - 0 Volunteer group accounting

- Personal Diaries of Time Usage
    - 0 Sorting mail
    - 0 Changing clothes
    - 0 Housework
    - 0 Work brought home from office

- Focus Groups
    - 0 Low amount of information processing tasks in home
    - 0 High need to manage money
    - 0 Conflicting perspective of family use of computing
    - 0 Education seen as best use
    - 0 Home task management
    - 0 Computer not a status symbol

Tasks Recommended for Sprite

- Use data from helpline to find difficulties in user interface
- Design consistent vocabulary for describing sprite interface
    - 0 Choose vocabulary from words used on helpline
- Make manual short and indexed by user tasks
- Lay out command sequences for user tasks and check for user perceived consistency

Tasks Recommended for Perky

- Define User
    - 0 Existing Economic Databases
    - 0 Focus Groups
        - Short Term User - Computer Co.
        - Mid Range User - France, Italy
        - Long Range User - Homebanking

- Define Templates
  - 0 Brainstorming/Focus Groups

- Run User Tests on Existing Software
  - 0 Mouse handling awkward
  - 0 Use threshold very high
  - 0 Graphics confusing
  - 0 Tutorial too fast
  - 0 Short animations very helpful
  - 0 Most detailed design decisions do not affect user unless they affect interface consistency

Five Years Later

- Computer Contract with Amiga signed
- Sales of Amiga sluggish and Star-tronics closed down
- Company officers opened new company selling redone version of Sprite to France and Italy

Case Study 2: The Blessing

Background Material

Organization: Chem Engineering Department
Software funded by National Science Foundation grant
Grant about to expire
Software already in use
Software in public domain
Distribution channels in place
Discretionary adoption of software hoped for

Description of Software Product

- Computer Aided Instruction System in Chem Engineering
- Allowed instructors to build graphics simulations of processes
- Simulations were driven by sets of equations
- Students had control over setting the values of the parameters in the equations

Human Factors Role

- Evaluate Software Product
- Recommend Changes to Design of Software
- Write Human Factors Evaluation for NSF Report

1. What areas of the Human Factors Software Lifecycle need to be addressed?

___ Defining User
___ Setting Functionality
___ Designing User Interface
___ Testing User Interface

Evaluation of CAI System

- Instructor interface complex and difficult to use
  - 0 Required considerable external memory
  - 0 Required detailed command sequences
  - 0 No immediate feedback on command sequences
  - 0 No recovery from basic errors

Evaluations of CAI System

- Student interface highly dependent on designed courseware
  - 0 Easy for students to get lost in sequence of screen displays
  - 0 Information on separate screens not integrated by student
  - 0 Students learning graphics manipulation not process concepts desired

0 Response time too slow to connect engineering process behavior to student's input

Consultant Recommendations

- Add editor to instructor interface
- Build and market courseware, not CAI package
- Build courseware templates for instructor use
- Read large body of literature on computer courseware design
- Run user tests on courseware

Five Years Later

- Editor borrowed from other source and built into software package
- Software not used
- New graphics-based computes supporting more sophisticated software
- Text book publishers beginning to market CAI courseware